DA SINGLE-PARENT FAMILIES

QUEST TO UNDERSTAND SELF AND MAKE SENSE OF INTIMATE RELATIONSHIPS WITH MEN

MERRYL J. CHOPRA

Mount Saint Vincent University

A thesis submitted to the
Department of Education
in partial fulfilment
of the requirements for the degree of
Masters of Arts in School Psychology
August, 1999

Printed in the United States of America.

Book Vine Press
2516 Highland Dr.
Palatine, IL 60067

Abstract

Much of human existence and the study of modem psychology have been centred around the changing Society within which we live. It is my belief that the early proponents in psychology may have been on to something when they proposed that mental activity was in some way linked to why we do the things we do. Modern psychology, nevertheless, which is primarily based in measurements and observations, tries to explain human nature by focusing on the external or outward behaviours of human existence. Freud said it best when he indicated that behaviour is merely the end result or the surface of what is rooted deeper within the crevices of our consciousness.

For decades many psychologists have studied the family and more specifically the single-parent family and claimed that single-parent families are "deviant" in nature. It is my intention for this thesis to change that perception, by offering or presenting single parents in a more positive light. This thesis, therefore, gives a voice to a few daughters who were raised by single mothers and attempts to understand how they saw themselves developing a sense of self within that context, as well as the impact their upbringing had on their ability to maintain intimate interpersonal relationships with men. I chose the single-parent family model as well as some aspects of their lived experiences to frame my inquiry.

Six women, raised by single mothers, between the ages of 18 and 35, were interviewed for this study. Participants' perceptions/schemas (socialization) were analyzed using the grounded theory framework. Six themes emerged from the analysis of the data. They are as follows:

1. Relationship with mother
2. The role that modelling plays in forming later relationships;
3. Participants' views on marriage

4. Trust in interpersonal relationships
5. Ease and comfort in forming and maintaining interpersonal intimate relationships with men
6. Self-reliance/ independence

Results from this study demonstrate that the development of self and the capacity for women who are raised by single moms to maintain interpersonal relations with men are based on a variety of factors and not just one singular concept. This study shows that how an individual experiences the world is based on many things, the personality they come to the world with, their strength of character, their lived experiences, what they learned from parents and family and society at large, the impressions and schemas they form along the way to make sense of the world around them, and how they perceive the world, manage and cope with the multiplicity of experiences they encountered on their journey. This study, therefore, concludes that the multitude of experiences that the women in this study had throughout their growth and development make them who they are. They are not what and who society claims them as being because they were raised by a single parent, "broken", "deviant", unstable and doomed to fail.

The findings of this study suggest a need to move beyond the preconceived notions that society has formed about single parent families and about their capacity to raise successful children. I believe that by wiping the slate clean, by erasing any preconceived notions or pre-existing ideas of what single parent families are or what and how they are capable of being, we can start fresh, and give them a fair break. Without the media saying and society perpetuating their existence without having met them, they will have a chance to just be whatever they are and choose to be. They can begin to accept themselves as they are, as authentic and genuine human beings, without necessarily relying on someone or a relationship (because someone said they should) to make them whole. It, therefore, goes without saying, that parents are not the sole contributor of their daughters (children) sense of self but rather, their daughter's sense of self is the total sum of their lived experiences.

Acknowledgements

A project of this magnitude required the hard work and dedication of many individuals. Therefore, I'd like to take this opportunity to thank the following people for their contribution to this work.

First, I am grateful to my advisor, Dr. Jane Gordon, who took a chance on me and really challenged me along the way to think beyond the lens I brought to her and to consider research I would never have considered on my own. She was my light and guide throughout this process. Dr Gordon's guidance, constant questioning, flexibility, presence, accommodation, encouragement and trust kept me moving forward. She was instrumental in seeing this project through to completion.

Dr. Blye Frank also deserves special acknowledgement as he was instrumental during the early stages of this project by educating me about the process, what was involved, what was needed, who I needed to talk to, participant selections and various methodologies to consider. His guidance was on point and made a big difference to this project and thesis defense.

I would also like to acknowledge my other committee members, Dr. Fred French and Dr. Olga Scibior for their interest in this project, support and constructive feedback.

Without the brave participants who stepped forward and openly shared their narratives with me this project would not be possible. I am filled with gratitude for their brevity and their courage.

I'd like to acknowledge my family, my husband, Neel, and my children, Alanah, Seth and Kaelyn, for their constant love and support each and every day. You are my rock! I am grateful everyday to have you in my life.

Dedication

I dedicate this body of work to my mother, who is, for the record, not "bad mother". She gave me the best of herself. She showered me with unconditional love early in my life and at a time when life seemed impossible for her. She was the first person who taught me how to love. The sacrifices she made for me will never go unnoticed. My love for her cannot be measured, bottled or contained. Thank you, mom, for giving me life and for your love.

And

To all single mothers and their daughters. Your narratives are strong, brave and heroic. Your personal story is your road map to your present existence. You alone can determine whether it defines you or not. You have the power to change society's definition and framing of you by reframing and rewriting your own story. It is my hope that you will find your own way of sharing your stories with the world.

Thank You

Contents

Chapter 1

Introduction

To understand and make sense of human
existence, theologians, philosophers, and
psychologists have dedicated much of their
lives to developing theories and hypotheses
which explain our meaning, our purpose, our
essence, and our existence. It is this author's
belief that some have already found the
answers, others are close and some are still
very far away. According to Gleitman (1991),
much of the development and popularization
of psychology, the definition of psychology
and the many psychological theories that are
now present in our society, can be credited
to a few early proponents in the field. They
are as follows: William James 1890; Wilhelm
Wundt, 1892; James Angel, 1910; John B.

Skinner, 1919; Kurt Koffka 1925; Arthur Gates, 1931; Norman Munn, 1951; Kenneth Clark and George Miller, 1970 and Richard Mayer, 1981.

Even the definition of psychology as it is known today has been subjected to many changes and revisions. During the course of its brief history, psychology has been described in many different ways. Early proponents in the field of psychology defined their field as 'the study' of "mental activity." However, at the turn of the century with the development of "behaviourism" and its concern for studying only the experiences that could be objectively measured, psychology was redefined as "the study of behaviour". Moreover, with the later development of cognition and phenomenological psychological theories, the definition of the discipline has been broadened to encompass both behaviour and mental processes (Gleitman, 1991).

Western psychology has primarily been situated in the scientific nature of human existence. Its aim has been to measure, observe and manipulate traits, behaviour, and actions in both humans and animals in an attempt to understand and make meaningful human existence in the context of their physical world.

Human interactions therefore, and the environmental contexts in which these interactions occur are said to be important in establishing and defining who we are in relationship to others and therefore, our identity. The many environmental contexts within which we are raised are supposed to provide a critical component to understanding an event or a person's experiences by providing clues which assist an individual in interpreting or perceiving who they are and the environment in which they find themselves, appropriately and successfully. An individual's lived experiences through social, cultural, and historical contexts, not only influence their perception of a particular experience, but mediate the deeper structures of identity development as well (Erikson, 1968).

Many western psychologists have, therefore, tried to centre their psychology within the constructs of the physical/ environmental world. They hold the belief that in order to make sense of why humans behave the way they do, they must compartmentalize and study segments of the population through, observations, questionnaires, deception, shock, brain waves, etc., and then measure these results via statistical tools and measurements. Their actions appear to suggest strongly that the answers to human nature lie outside of the very humans they study.

Existential/humanistic psychologists hold an opposing view to those described above. Their theories of human development which states that the development of self is based on internal, innate forces that propel an individual to act, have been criticized by many; particularly their American counterparts. They assert that the perceptions we hold and the choices we make based on our becoming or emerging in the physical environment, are responsible for our later psychological turmoil (Maslow, 1954; May, Alport, Feifel, Maslow & Rogers, 1961).

Furthermore, these theorists indicated that in order to obtain an accurate enough picture of an individual, we must set aside many of our beliefs, perceptions and reconceived notions of what we have learned and instead focus completely on the individual we are getting to know. It has also been asserted that by letting the individual tell their story, truly and authentically without our projection of thoughts, judgements, criticism, etc., can we truly help individuals in search of self. The many perceptions and beliefs about reality that many of us hold, are said to distort our judgements. Therefore, it is essential that we help the individual realize and see past these distortions. The core of their existence lies within them, not outside them with their behaviours and actions. The force, the drive, the internal processing and decision making is what is responsible for our overt actions and reactions to the environment (Maslow, 1954; May, Allport, Feifel Maslow & Rogers, 1961).

Existentialists differentiate between three simultaneous aspects within which each individual identifies their place in the world. The first is called the environment, or the "world-around", the biological world. The second is the world of humans, the "with world"; and finally, the relationship to ourselves, the "own-world". All organisms, humans as well as animals, are said to have the first world which is environment. The struggles that humans are said to confront constantly are less so in the biological world but are in the world of inter-personal relationships with others, the ''with-world'' (Maslow, 1954; May, Allport, Feifel Maslow & Rogers, 1961).

The way we make sense and understand others in the world is determined by our relationship with them. Existential psychologists hold the belief that,

> We cannot accept any human group around us…Animals have an environment, we have a world, and this world includes the meaning of these other people to us… Whether they are members

of our family or friends, loved ones, people we can trust, whether they are hostile, or are our enemies (May, 1967, pp. 5-6)."

How we identify and draw meaning from this group, and others in the world, depends on how we put ourselves into it. We could never experience or accept people in the world as friends, unless we commit ourselves to friendship. Therefore, human love can never be understood on purely biological/social and cultural plains but inevitably depends upon a personal choice, a decision, and commitment to the other person (Fromm, 1956; May, 1967).

Beginning as fetuses, in our mother's womb, humans are surrounded by an environment that tries to foster their development, growth, and survival (biological world). Their nourishment and comfort depend heavily on what mothers ingest and the ways in which they physically position their bodies and themselves. When born into the physical world, newborns are introduced to a new environment which they have to learn about, become familiar with and adapt to. This new environment involves people, thoughts, perceptions, psychology (interpersonal world). As newborns, the degree with which the internalization of environmental influences take place, is slow. Nevertheless, infancy marks a period of increased growth and development, where all of the earlier exposures still apply but a higher form of interaction between mother/ primary caregiver is evidenced. As the infant grows, more and more of their neural pathways are connected, their muscles and joints strengthen, they move from crawling to holding on to things in an effort to support themselves. They eventually become strong enough to walk independently. They also become more vocal as they develop speech. In the interim, they are learning about human behaviour through observation, modelling and teaching. Eventually they get old enough to play with friends, go to school, and later become adults while also developing a sense of self (Santrock, 1996).

A wave of developmental theorists emerged during the past century. These theorists have all tried to make sense of an individual's development of self through a variety of ways. The early proponents in psychology appeared to have laid their mark by the number of individuals who have since developed theories in support of their claims or in opposition of it. Some of these new theorists are as follows: Guidubali, Perry & Natasi, 1985; Biller & Bahm, 1971; Amato, 1991; Mott, Kowaleski-Jone, Menaghan, 1991, Santrock, 1970; Lynn & Sawrey, 1959; Bandura, 1977; Belsky, 1989; Amato, 1995; Biller & Weiss, 1970; Hunt & Hunt, 1977; Hetherington, 1972. Many of these theorists' have tried to understand human behaviour and development by focusing on the family unit, parenting and the effects it has on a child's later development.

Parenting, has been a widely studied topic not only in psychology but in other related fields as well. Because parenting does not come with a manual that explain all of the "Do's" and "Don'ts", the tools and skills required to raise a child, it remains an elusive phenomenon. Furthermore, since every individual is unique and is raised with their own set of "know hows", a single definition of parenting could not satisfy nor apply to an entire human race.

The family, and child-rearing practices in Canada have undergone intense changes from the large extended family during the hunting and gathering era to the smaller, more isolated nuclear family of the 1950s. This evolution has also changed the dynamic of the family unit. A move was made from a more flexible family system during the hunting-gathering years to a more rigid family structure of the 1950s. Today, society appears to shift back and forth between flexible family systems to more rigid ones. (Mandell & Duffy, 1995; Baker, 1996; Eichler, 1988). "Family" changes as society changes and family in Canada at present is marked by a diversity of family structures inconceivable to many. For instance, family consists of the joint, traditional couple custody arrangements, single motherhood, single fatherhood, blended and units, extended, lesbian, gay and straight. Children are raised in each of these environment (Eichler, 1988; Kaschak, 1992).

There may be many reasons why the family unit and structure are changing today. Actually, it may not even be changing necessarily but rather growing out of the restrictive definition the government and society have used to define "family". Among the major structural changes is the growth of single-parent headed households. Divorce has been hailed as one of the major contributors to single-headed households today. It is likely that almost half of the nation's children will live in a single-parent household before the age of 18. Researchers studying the effects of children raised in single-parent families found evidence which demonstrates both positive (Jenkins, 1988; Morrison, 1995) and negative outcomes to this type of arrangement (Amato, 1995; Mandell & Duffy,1995; AbeIsohn & Saayman, 1991; Forehand, McCombs, Long, Brody &

Fauber, 1988; Hetherington, Stanley-Hagan & Anderson, 1989).

In an age of information overload, it is difficult to determine which theories should receive full attention and which a peruse. At the same time, one must try to consider as many aspects of an individual or individuals' life experiences in order to make sense of it. Many developmental theorists have composed theories in an attempt to try to understand and make sense of human development. They have generally found that secure attachments to caregivers are essential to children's psychological and social adjustment (Belsky, 1989; Erikson, 1968, Freud, 1933; Bowlby, 1982, 1989).

More recent researchers investigating women's development have made some very interesting discoveries (Gilligan, 1991; Kaplan & Klein, 1991; Baker Miller, 1991; Surrey, 1991). They found that the differential treatment of girls from birth to puberty have contributed to many of the problems faced by adolescents. This new theory (Self-in-Relation theory) asserts that girls' sense of self is formed or linked to the relationships they form and develop. Relationship is seen as the basic goal of development. The Self-in-Relation theory assumes that other aspects of self, such as creativity, autonomy, and assertion develop within this primary context. Girl's relational skills are said to be fostered from birth with their mothers, the primary caregiver, modelling, though perhaps not consciously, relational skills as their daughters progress through the life stages.

The Social Learning theory also asserts that children model their behaviour on how adults respond to them although this theory preceded the Self-In-Relation theory (Bandura, 1977). Childhood is seen as the time when children are developing their behavioural and emotional skills and use their interactions with significant adults, such as their mother to establish coping skills. They are said to learn primarily through imitation (Schroeder,1992; Santrock, 1992; Landers, 1996; Myers, 1989).

With so many differing views of human development, how then can we fully explain what causes people to do the things they do or which effects will be long lasting and which ones short-lived? In recognition of the importance of context for making an accurate and successful interpretation of any life experience, this thesis attempts to examine the single parent, mother-headed household, with which to foster deeper meaning and understanding of their daughters' development of self and their capacity to form and sustain interpersonal intimate relationships with men.

Existential/humanistic psychologists and philosophers seem to suggest that human beings to some extent are in control of their own destiny. Their capacity to form interpersonal relationships are only as meaningful as what they bring to it or how they place themselves in it (May, 1967, Allport, 1961; Feifęl, 1961; Maslow, 1961; Rogers, 1961).

In keeping with the existential and humanistic beliefs, this author seeks to make sense of the development of self as well as daughters of single mothers' capacity to maintain intimate interpersonal relationships with men. The author did this by investigating how potential impressions/ schemas and perceptions are formed based on a variety of lived experiences and choices that these women make during the span of their development, in an attempt to gain an understanding of what has led them to do the things they did and make the choices they made thus far in relation to the topics under investigation. Therefore, the single parent family as well as certain aspects of participants' lived experiences within this context were used as the backdrop from which to frame the inquiry.

Further, the author seeks to allow the themes that the participants provided to present themselves as authentically and as fully as possible using the Grounded Theory theoretical framework. A discussion section is included which attempts to synthesize and make sense of the data by pulling it together as a whole while incorporating some of the literature review and insights gained during the process.

Chapter 2

Literature Review

To understand the evolution and conception of single parenting in Canada, a brief history of the construction of family and family dynamic is presented. A review of some of the psychological literature looking at certain aspects of human development is also presented in the form of a quasi-debate as to which theories come the closest to my beliefs and why. It is hoped that by integrating these different schools of thought, one would get a glimpse of how society, and thus the family, has changed over time, as well as learn about how some psychological theories, as selected by the researcher, try to make sense of human development.

Historical Background of Families in Canada

With the ever changing and evolving structure of the Canadian "family", it is not surprising that many scholars spend much of their time researching the nature of the changing dynamic of "family" in Canada (Mandell & De7 2995). Forms and compositions as well as socially approved responsibilities have changed over time.

Up to this point in time, the most dominant perspective on the family was the traditional notion, from the 1940s -1970s, which emphasized that "the family " was the basic institution of society. It was seen as both an economic and a social unit. A family consisted of two adults of the opposite sex who shared economic resources, sexual intimacy, labour, accommodation, reproduction, and child-rearing, and provided each other with companionship, assistance, love and respect, heirs, and social status (Mandell & Duffy 1995; Havas, 1995; DeVault, 1991).

Economic Interdependence

During the hunting and gathering era, families were large and involved cooperative work with men, women, and children. Women and children looked after farm duties and the everyday running of the households while the husbands, if not working the farm, were away hunting (Mandell & Duffy, 1995; Baker, 1996; Havas, 1995).

As immigrants settled in Canada, a shift occurred from the small scale farming communities to large scale agriculture. The fur trade also played a big part in this changing lifestyle. With industries being created and more and more factories being built, families and others were forced to relinquish their farms and seek work elsewhere. Working close to home had now become a thing of the past; and travel to and from the family home, for great distances to find work, was now the more viable option for which many families succumbed. Economic interdependence now determined family structures. As a result of industrialization, families became a more specialized unit with more of a focus on procreation, child-rearing, consumption, and affection; and, instead of both mothers and fathers contributing to the family financially, roles were divided. Mothers took on the duty of the household and care taking of the children, while men worked outside of the home and were considered the "breadwinners" of the family. Families were no longer egalitarian in nature. They became units that were primarily governed by men because they now supplied the money to take care of the household (DeVault, 1991; Mandell & Duffy, 1995; Baker, 1996).

Structure and Ideology

The size of the family was also affected. Canadians in the 1870s lived in more extended family settings. They resided in homes averaging 5.4 people which included, husbands, wives, children, and dependent elderly relations. Due to the changing labour force and the urbanization of societies, households became smaller, more specialized, and more isolated (Mandell & Duffy, 1995).

The 1950 s marked the era of the nuclear family which was created by the middle class. This new idealized version of the "perfect family" consisted of the stay-at-home mom with at least two children and an employed husband. Most women were now expected to work in the home and thus were not encouraged to work outside of the home because it was not perceived as the "proper" thing to do. It would reflect negatively on the family and would harm the children and her husband. Women seem to have accepted this new family ideal by becoming engrossed in the running of the home. Their focus or role shifted to coordinating family projects. Household chores, also became one of their primary duties and responsibility. For the men who worked outside the home, home became a domestic retreat, a sanctuary of intimacy against the harsh reality of the workplace (Mandell & Duffy, 1995). Not all women were fortunate or unfortunate enough, depending on what point of view one takes, to stay at home. Single mothers, arising from widowhood or desertion, often had to obtain paid work outside of the home to support their families. These women were looked down upon by the upper class and were viewed as "misfits" by the wider society (Mandell & Duffy,1995; Baker, 1996).

Since the emergence of the women's movement, in the 1960s and 1970s, more and more women have entered the labour force, including married women, who about 50 years ago, would have been looked down upon, shunned or criticized for doing so. Today, married women as well as single women seek paid employment outside of the home and continuously strive to find a work-life balance between the combination of employment and family duties and responsibilities (Mandell & Duffy, 1995; Baker, 1996; Havas, 1995). On the contrary, and to emphasize the changing times, married men are now seen more often engaging in domestic labour and childcare as their partners involvement in the labour force has shifted the load more equitably between the spouses. (Mandell & Duffy, 1995).

Defining Family

As society changes so does the family. Eichler (1988) noted that the notion of "family" is not static. It is forever changing, becoming more and more complex and dynamic. Eichler vehemently asserts that society, Canada, or the government should abandon the idea of the monolithic family, which is the assumption that one dimension carries over to all other dimensions. For example, it is assumed that a married couple will inevitably have children together or that any children present are the biological children of the married couple. The monolithic model assumes that family is a linear entity, where the variable A, will undoubtedly result in variable B (Eichler, 1988).

Eichler (1988) further noted that the definitions used for family in Canadian research and policy making are old and one-dimensional. They do not include or are not up to date with the changing family dynamic. According to Statistics Canada, the family unit consists of a married couple with or without never-married children or a single parent living together with never-married children. The children can be any age as long as they have never been married. According to the government, cohabitating couples who have lived together for longer than one year are considered to be married. This does not, however, apply to same sex couples because only heterosexual couples can legally marry (Mandell & Duffy,1995). However, the latter view is under scrutiny and review and change may be on the way in the near future.

Statistics Canada also uses the term "economic family" to refer to people who are related by blood, marriage, or adoption and are sharing the same living space. It is also interesting to note that previously married children who got a divorce and moved back in with their parents, were not considered a part of the family according to the government (Mandell & Duffy, 1995).

Therefore, Eichler (1988), proposes that, due to the very nature of its diversity and plurality, Canada needs to adopt a multidimensional approach to family organization and structure. Definitions of what constitutes a family have enlarged, focusing more on what families do, rather than what they look like. Instead of having laws and morals define "family", if indeed family must be labelled something, one must look for the commonalities in the many variations that society has now come to view as family (Mandell & Duffy, 1995; Havas, 1995).

Single parenting is one of many ways in which the Canadian society has had to redefine "the family" in recent times. A myriad of other forms and structures have also revolutionized how we see family. In this complex and multifaceted society, we are faced with dual earners who make-up the traditional version of the family; there is also the never married category; the post-divorce; the blended; the gay and lesbian, as well as the extended family who are co-existing with traditional families. Within all of the aforementioned definitions, further division is needed in order to accurately define each category (Eichler,

1988). It is therefore unrealistic to continue to abide by a traditional version of what family is or should be since that version no longer exist (Eichler, 1988; Mandell & Duffy, 1995; Havas, 1995). The ever changing and diverse notion or experience of the family has grown so enormously that a single definition may soon be impossible. Definitions, however, do not speak to the functionality of the family, but rather provides a label for further categorization, separation, isolation, scrutiny and judgment.

It is almost five decades now since the era of the nuclear family and there have been many debates as to whether it has led to the privatization and the individualization of families in Canada. It has been widely argued that the nuclear family model provided the basis within which the government laid the standards for providing support to families. Families who did not fit this model were considered outcasts and were viewed as immoral. They were refused support because of their "deviant nature" or non-compliance with traditional models (Mandell & Duffy, 1995).

According to Havas (1995), "the family as ideology denies that what happens in the wider society affects all our children and gives the illusion that we can somehow isolate ourselves (p. 71)." It makes the responsibility of child-rearing a private one and it denies the view that any child's disadvantage, ultimately affects other children and the society at large. Thus, each parent fights to obtain the best for their children, more or less reinforcing the anti-social nature of the current family structure. Bonds are formed with some family members while others are ignored or excluded. This creates a justification for a lack of adequate social and family policy. It also establishes a situation where parents objectify their children by placing them in competitive situations without even consciously realizing it. This takes away from the instinctual and unconditional love for all children because parents who fight for access to services for their own children, often view the gains of other children as taking from their own. This notion fits within the capitalist's framework and within a larger economic context.

With families so isolated and singular there is little accountability for the actions of a family or community. Each family unit seem to exist in its own vacuum or on its own planet and affords little consideration for what is happening outside of that realm. The government thus continues to support the notion of the traditional family model ignoring the diversification of what is currently happening amidst it (Mandell & Duffy, 1995; Havas, 1995).

Family, as it exists today, fits a very broad and dynamic definition in spite of its prevailing roots. The current family make up is not singular by any means; families come in many sizes, types, and colours. However, more and more of the literature is focusing on the changing trends of the family, particularly on the "broken family" (Mandell & Duffy, 1995). There have been much debate on the ever increasing number of single-parent families, most of which are attributed to divorce (Amato, 1995; Mandell

& Duffy, 1995; Abelsohn & Saayman, 1991; Forehand, McCombs, Long, Brody & Fauber, 1988; Hetherington, Stanley-Hagan & Anderson, 1989).

Divorce

Divorce has been described as the number one leading cause of the dissolution of the family (Mandell & Duffy, 1995; Baker, 1996; Ambert, 1980). It has been on the rise in Canada for more than three decades. This increase in the rate of divorce began in the late 1960's and early 1970's with the change in divorce laws in 1968. With more relaxed divorce laws the divorce rate climbed dramatically and continued to do so each year until the 1990's, where it levelled off. The estimated rate of Canadian marriages that undoubtedly ended in divorce during the 1980's was one in five (Ambert, 1980). These rising divorce rates were alarming and caused great concerns for the Canadian family. The rate of increase was dramatic between 1970 and 1986, rising from a low of 18.6 percent to a high of 43.1 percent. In 1987, the divorce rate reached its highest peak in history; fifty percent of all marriages resulted in divorce. At present, it has been estimated that for every ten Canadian marriages, four or more are expected to end in divorce. Though the numbers still remain high, the 1990s have seen a slight decline in divorce rates and there appears to be a levelling off (Maccoby, 1990; Mandell & Duffy,1995).

Nonetheless, it is believed that about 84 percent of Canadian women are expected to spend a large proportion of their lives in husbandless households where they will have to support themselves and often their children. Consequently, divorce is the single largest precipitator of single parent families in Canada. Divorce also marks a time of change where many different issues must be worked out; for example, when children are involved, custody arrangements are necessary, support guidelines must be arranged and enforced, economic consequences as a result of the divorce becomes real, remarriage is another issue to be considered, maintaining an acceptable lifestyle for both parties of divorce as well as for the child(ren) of divorce are other issues that must be considered. It is a radical life change for everyone involved (Ambert, 1980; Mandell & Duffy, 1995; Abelsohn & Saayman, 1991; Forehand, McCombs, Long, Brody & Fauber, 1988).

Divorce, historically, has carried negative connotations and continues to do so today. It is viewed as wrong, immoral, dysfunctional and disruptive of family life. These views are based on the so-called desirable family structure as noted above. Recently, there has been a shift in the perceptions of many who are in the field of research and health care to realize that divorce can be a beneficial and necessary aspect of one's life. For an unhappy marriage, riddled with pain, suffering, abuse, etcetera, whether it be emotional or physical, can be more detrimental to one's physical, emotional and mental well-being. In such a situation, divorce may be in many ways the cure to a bad ailment which have been suppressed and covered up for many years due to fears, worries, judgment, alienation and isolation (Ambert, 1980).

As a result of the increase in the divorce rate in the late 1960's and early 1970's, many of the nation's children were raised in a single-parent household for at least a portion of their lives. Close to 60 percent of divorcing couples had children below 18 years of age; representing a total sum of 30,000 children who were involved in divorce each year in Canada (Ambert, 1980).

The impact of divorce on children's lives has been widely studied. The research spans many aspects of a child's life including, discipline, education, psychological and social well-being, delinquency, health, adjustment, deviance, etcetera, to name just a few (Hansein &, Heins, Julian, & Sussman 1995; Gately & Schwebel 1995; Guidubali, Perry & Natasi, 1985; Asmussen Larsen, 1991; Amato, 1987; Hetherington et al., 1989).

Children's lives do change drastically as a result of a divorce and so do the lives of their parents. Children often become confused and overwhelmed as their environment suddenly and abruptly changes. It can be a difficult and overwhelming situation to wrap their head around and make sense of. Everything that was once secure, familiar and comfortable is no more; their lives are uprooted and they watch the unraveling of it without having much say or control. They are forced to adjust to a new way of experiencing life, a new way of living. The transition from a divorce can be very tumultuous for families and it can be unsettling and destabilizing for a period of time.

Children often receive ambiguous messages from their separated caregivers who are also trying to put the pieces of their lives back together. Their parenting styles may change since they no longer have to confer with another one another. One parent may become more authoritarian while the other may become more permissive. These adjustments in behaviours do not always remain stable over time; i.e., they change as parents deal with the divorce or meet new people who may influence their lives. Children in turn have to relearn and unlearn the changing moods and roles of their new parent(s), making their lives more confusing

(Hansein, Heins, Julian & Sussman, 1995; Gately, Schwebel, 1995).

Single-Parent Families

In its simplest form a single-parent refers to a household in which an adult raises children alone without the living presence or daily assistance from a second adult. Single-parent homes may be the result of divorce, the death of a spouse or a parent who has never married.

Variations of single-parenting exist as well, for example, there is custodial parenting, joint custody agreements, and extended family caregivers. A custodial parent for example, is one in which one parent is given full legal responsibility for the child(ren). They take care of a child's day-to-day activities but may choose to share the parenting role with an ex-spouse, either on the weekends or during the week. The parenting duties in this situation may span over two households, where the time the child(ren) spends with each parent varies. Extensive access, where child(ren) have almost equal time with each parent, increases the opportunity to maintain a stable relationship and bond.

Joint custody arrangements involve the legal responsibility of a shared parenting role and may vary in the degree to which each provides physical, psychological and financial support. It is somewhat similar to the extensive access parenting situation described above, in that, both parents share as equal as possible the parenting duties. Although in this case, both parents are required by law to adhere to this arrangement. Financial concerns may or may not be an issue in either model depending on the amount or quality of support the child is receiving or the parents have available.

Another example of the diversity of single parenting includes a single-parent living in a household with their child(ren) where other adults are present. These other adults may include grandparents, aunts, uncles, or close friends creating an extended family environment. The single-parent in such a household may elicit and receives support from the other members of the household. This dwelling situation can create a supportive and less burdensome parenting experience. In addition, the child(ren) in such an environment are likely exposed to various adults with varying skills and abilities from whom they can learn, receive support and gain additional role models (Amato, 1995; Amato & Keith, 1991; Eichler, 1988; Mandell, Duffy, 1988). I am, nonetheless, interested in the single-parent model with a female-head who has had no or little support or contact over a number of years with a consistent male partner.

Although society is at a point where about half of the children born today will eventually live in a single-parent household before the age of 18, single-parenting still continues to be viewed as "broken", unstable or doomed for failure. This notion pathologizes the single-parent family and treats them as a problem that needs to be remedied. Moreover, it tends to create guilt in divorcing or separating parents in addition to the blame it elicits from the community and others at large (Stable, 1990).

The extensive research literature, over the last few decades, suggests that children of single-parent families are more likely to exhibit significant problems than children from two-parent families. These problems include behavioural difficulties (such as, aggression, burglary, lying, temper tantrums, disobedience, running away, alcohol and illicit drug use, promiscuity, etc.), psychological problems (for example, low self-esteem, depression, and withdrawal) and difficulties in the education system (such as truancy and underachievement). Furthermore, some studies have indicated that single-parenthood is correlated with unhealthy psychological, social, and intellectual development (Owusu-Bempah, 1995).

Socio-psychological research emphasizes children's social, emotional, and intellectual well-being. Such research evidence suggests that children of divorce or separated parents do worse than children of intact families throughout the life cycle: As adults they seem to have lower educational attainment (McLanahan, 1985), earn less income, are more likely to be dependent on the welfare system, are more likely to bear a child out of wedlock (McLanahan & Burgess, 1988), get divorced (Glenn & Kramer, 1987) and to be the head of a single-parent family (McLanahan, 1988; Amato, 1987; Amato & Keith, 1991a; Glenn & Kramer, 1985; Tennant, 1988). In addition, studies show that children who lose a parent through separation, divorce or desertion are more likely to be vulnerable to acute psychiatric disturbance as children and adults, avoid marriage, experience divorce and are susceptible to various other psychiatric disorders (Amato & Keith, 1991b).

Further research has suggested that much of the increased poverty found among children in recent years is as a direct result of the increase in single-parenthood. The behaviour of single-parents that influence deviance and low achievement outcomes are said to stem mainly from the understandable tendency of single parents to give autonomy to their children too early, when they are often too young to handle it. Although it is said that single-parenthood causes poverty and reduces the quality of parenting, it is poor parenting as well as poverty that are believed to be responsible for the future generation of single parents. These single parents, in turn, are expected to join the welfare system (Dornbusch, Hieman, & Lin, 1996). The western world continues to hold its traditional two-parent family as the ideal growth environment for a child(ren)'s development and, therefore, the findings of many of the above research studies and the conclusions drawn from them are not surprising (Owusu-Bempah, 1995).

There is a large body of research on single-parent families today that describes them as pathological in nature (Dornbusch, Hieman, & Lin, 1996; Amato & Keith, 1991b; McLanahan, 1985; McLanahan, 1988; Amato, 1987; Amato & Keith, 1991a; Glenn & Kramer, 1985; Tennant, 1988). With this bombardment of research which feeds into the popular Media airways, forming and further perpetuating the negative stereotypes about single-parent families, it is not surprising that the research that represents single-parents in a positive light recedes quietly into the background, receiving little attention or even an acknowledgment (Dornbusch, Hieman, & Lin,1996; Amato & Keith, 1991b; McLanahan, 1985; McLanahan, 1988; Amato, 1987; Amato & Keith, 1991a; GIenn & Kramer, 1985; Tennant, 1988).

Nevertheless, research on successful single-parent families do exist (Morrison 1995; Jenkins, 1988; Shireman, 1996). Below, you will find research that explores a number of factors that help demonstrate possible contributors to successful single-parent families. For instance, the age and maturity level of the single-parent is one consideration. Other factors include educational level and level of commitment to the family. Even though financial matters have surfaced as a possible concern, many single-parents indicated that due to this hardship they have had to learn to budget and work within the limits of their financial restraints. In addition, many parents noted that they faced fewer obstacles as a single-parent than as a dual-parent and as a result their children experienced more consistency in their parenting style with less competing values to juggle. Successful single-parents also equated their success to their accomplishments and the healthy relationships they were able to form with their children. They indicated that they had to work harder in order to become more successful. Many of these parents, because of their strong commitment to their families and children, are willing to overcome whatever hurdles came their way in order to fight against the odds of what society has predicted for them. Flexibility, also became a key asset for them, as they had to learn to manage and organize different schedules. Parents and children alike often became more resilient by finding new and creative ways to cope and support one another.

Morrison (1995) and Jenkins (1988) work on successful single-parent families, found that children interviewed, described their experiences of being raised by a single mother as stable rather than unstable. For example, the conflicts that most children of divorce once faced became significantly reduced and they reported experiencing more peace in their homes. Many of these children noted that they had a greater capacity to form better relationships with both parents. Many described their time spent with their single-parent as quality time because previously much of their parents' time were often spent working. Furthermore, the relationship that formed between the child and their single-parent was described as more mature. It seemed more equal in that their parents confided in them more and they often reciprocated. The children also noted that they developed responsibility early on because they played an active part in the family decision making process. They also shared household responsibilities such as chores and meal preparations appropriate to their age (Morrison, 1995; Jenkins, 1988).

The concerns over the increase in divorce and the major results of psychological maladjustment (such as, poor school performance and delinquency) that is said to arise from single-parenting in all areas of society are grave (Goode, 1992; Haskey, 1990). The increase in single-parent families is not unique to Canada or the United States. Bradshaw and Miller (1991) reported that the United Kingdom had over one million single-parent families, or, put another way, one in seven families was headed by a single-parent. They predicted that as many as one-third of all children in Britain will experience life in a single-parent family. Similarly, Roll (1992) reported that single-parent families with children under the age of 18 ranged from 5 - 6 percent in Greece, Italy, and Spain to over 17 percent in Britain. In both Britain and Australia, greater problems were found to exist with either children of single parents or among the mothers themselves (Haskey, 1990; Kierman & Wicks, 1990). Kierman and Wicks (1990) predicted that by the year 2000 only half of all children will have spent all their lives in a conventional two-parent family.

On the basis of this research, children's problems following marital breakdown such as delinquency and educational difficulties are readily attributed to single-parenthood itself. The custodial parent thus becomes the object of blame for their child(ren)'s behaviour. This extends to professional childcare workers who tend to respond in a similar fashion when dealing with single-parent families. The frequent references to single-parent families as poor families, families with problems, or plainly, problem families, have connotations of low social status and a negative image (Hardey & Crow, 1991).

If children of single-parents are at an increased risk and if this is to be prevented then a crucial issue to be addressed is the basis of their vulnerability. Since not all children of single-parent families are "damaged", and many succeed extremely well, it is important to identify the "characteristics" of high-risk children.

A meta-analysis of 92 studies found modest support only for marital conflict in accounting for the range of emotional, academic, social, and general behavioural problems commonly associated with children of single-parent families (Amato & Keith, 1991a; Emery, 1982). With only modest support for marital conflict as a contributor for the difficulties children face after divorce or separation, other factors must also play a role. One possibility is the quality and quantity of information about the absent parent a child receives; in that, knowledge of the connectedness is believed to lead to the general well-being of children (Brodinsky, 1990). Bharat (1988) suggests that children in single-parent families felt a sense of loss regarding the absent father.

Another factor may be the ongoing struggles that single parents have in creating a new identity. They struggle with finding where they fit and belong, how to set boundaries and rules because they are alone and have very little positive role models to compare themselves to. There is little positive representation of the single-parent family in the media. Television programs or movies often portray the more traditional nuclear family model and they do so more often in a positive light, while on the other hand, single-parent families are often shown from a more pathological standpoint. Television more often show that the way to overcome the dire straits of single-parenthood is to find a new mate and remarry and live happily ever after. Some examples from television are as follows: Jerry McGuire and As Good As It Gets. Print media on the other hand, often report on ways of overcoming the pathology of the single-parent family. Single parents, therefore, must invent or create their own rules of engagement which are said to be generated from within their own context and not from a context they cannot quite relate to. There are no models to follow in which to compare and learn from, to accept or reject (Morrison, 1995). Similar concerns have been voiced by children of single-parent households. Many find that having exposure to only one opinion or model is limiting; and makes it difficult when trying to develop appropriate ways of relating to others.

Having reviewed the literature of the family, funneling it so it ends with the topic of focus (single parenting), one now has a sense of the practical nature of the construction of the family. Nevertheless, this review does not provide deep insights as to the interpersonal relating and the development of self in the individuals' that construct the family unit. Since it is the author's interest to learn about the development of self in the context of being raised in a single parent family and its impact on interpersonal intimate relationships, a survey of some of the psychological literature pertaining to an individual's psychological development of self is warranted.

A section of literature surveyed focused primarily on the development of children raised in single parent families, presenting them as being adversely affected by the disenfranchising of the typical family construct. There were very few studies found that presented single parent families as successful and positive. The few that were found could be counted on one hand.

A review of some of the more traditional theories of development were also inserted, as well as one, more recent, theory to provide a more global development of self, other than the ones that pertained just to the children of "broken families". The selection of theories, though not entirely purposeful, made for an interesting review and debate. I hold the belief that an individual's self is a constant phenomenon which is always present; it is a universal self and therefore has no gender, race or colour; to become aware of this self and to develop this self, one has to be present to it and open to the Who, the Where, the What, the Why and the How they are doing the things they are. This is not a viewable self, a replicable self, it cannot be seen, touch, or felt. It can only be experienced from within. It is internally driven, providing individuals with clues, instincts, intuitions, hunches, gut feelings, a "force" for us to know and to choose to act in one way or another. It is not externally based and cannot be measured or observed. I chose to, therefore, provide in the section that follows a brief glimpse of some of the theories that may be in opposition to my way of thinking and some that came close to a theory of self that is likened to my own point of view.

Psychological Developmental Theories

Many psychological theories have been proposed over the past century to explain children's biological, social, and psychological development. Some theories study males while others study females and still, others do both. Miller (1991) discusses the necessity of developing new language and new concepts to describe women's unique experiences and points to the problems that arise when principles of male development are cast as universal principles of human development. Women in Western society have been said to be merely "carriers" of certain aspects of the human experience. With the exclusion of females from early studies which was supposed to determine basic human characteristics, a common set of traits were observed in males which were later generalized to fit all people (Hyde, 1996). Society has therefore been over-taxed with the many male characteristics that is supposed to lead to life's successes.

Hence, in order to fully understand human development, there needs to be a thorough demonstration of both female and male experiences as well as their interactions with one another (Gilligan, 1991; Kaplan & Klein, 1991; Miller, 1991; Surrey, 1991). The following theoretical perspectives are offered to illustrate this current state of affairs in the field of psychological development.

According to Amato (1995), children's development is closely linked to and are affected by the number of adults who are part of their immediate circle or environment, as well as the quantity and quality of resource they provide. The immediate adult circle or environment refers to those adults who interact with the children on a regular basis and who are psychologically pronounced for them. Resources, Amato describes, are assets or interpersonal processes that have beneficial consequences for children. These positive consequences include the development of cognitive, behavioural, and social skills, good physical health, a subjective sense of well-being, a positive self-image, the ability to exercise a degree of self-control, and the attainment of valued social statuses.

In addition, some developmental psychologists have noted that secure attachments to caregivers are essential to children's psychological and social adjustment (Belsky, 1989). Imitation Theory also states that children are more likely to attend to and imitate adults for whom they have affection and admiration (Bandura, 1977). Children are constantly evaluating their own behaviours in relation to the individuals they admire; thus, significant others, are said to have major influences on children's development (Amato, 1995).

Amato (1995) notes that having one close primary relationship may be enough to ensure that a child achieves a basic sense of security, a positive sense of self and some degree of happiness, but having close relationships with others grant additional benefits to children for a number of reasons: Two adults can provide more affection, practical assistance and supervision than one; an additional adult is likely to add to the existing knowledge and skills that the other does not have. This individual could add to the range of behaviour and ideas that children may learn through teaching, learning, modeling and observation. If one adult is unable to carry out the everyday parenting skills, the other can step in; being a single parent can be both physically and psychologically draining. On the other hand, in dual family situations, one adult can provide support for the other and the child sees that, therefore, an imprint or an impression is made and with this observation an schema is built within them for later recall and modelling. Two adults can provide models for desirable social behaviours, such as, cooperation, sharing, negotiation, compromise, and the amicable resolution of disagreements. These behaviours require the presence of another individual. Single-parent families by definition do not have this additional support to draw from and are therefore at a disadvantage. Furthermore, Amato (1995) noted that, "two-parent families provide a more unitary form of authority in areas of decision making and discipline (pp. 22-23)."

Much of the research in support of the above findings and assumptions have focused primarily on boys' adjustment to divorce and custody issues, such as being raised by single mothers with the absence of a consistent male figure. The research findings have generally been similar. Boys are said to have more of a difficult time adjusting to the divorce setting than girls. For example, studies show that boys become more aggressive, are more dependent, are more likely to become delinquents, and are more likely to experience difficulty with school work; and the lack of consistent contact with a father figure is said to likely hinder the identification or the modelling process and, thus, results in problems in "normal" sex-role development (Guidubali, Perry & Natasi, 1985; Biller & Bahm, 1971; Amato, 1991; Mott, Kowaleski-Jone, Menaghan, 1991, Santrock 1970; Lynn & Sawrey, 1959).

The few studies that have been done with a focus on females' adjustment to divorce and coping with an absent parent (father) are somewhat dated (Biller & Weiss, 1970; Hunt & Hunt, 1977; Hetherington, 1972; Santrock, 1970). Nevertheless, their findings revealed that girls experience as many problems with adjustment to a single-parent lifestyle as do boys. Girls tend to internalize their feelings and perceptions and are more likely to fall under the radar and go undetected; whereas boys do the reverse; they externalize their fears, worries and upsets, thus, making their reactions more obvious, blatant, loud and more easily detectable. Further, it was found that for girls, the lack of a constant adult male presence was related to a lack of skills in interaction with men and may also be related to sexual misconduct, and inappropriate assertiveness with peers.

Researchers who work extensively in the area of role identification have suggested that because of a father's differential treatment of boys and girls, he is seen as the most important figure in the, "reciprocal sex-role learning of offspring of either sex (p. 25) (Johnson, 1965 as cited in Hetherington, 1972)."

Hetherington (1972), states that gender identity is generally established somewhere between an infant's twelfth and eighteenth month and is well in place by the third year of life. Although there are no significant gender-related differences in newborns themselves, both mothers and fathers tend to rate female children as being much softer, smaller, have finer-features, and are less alert. Fathers were noted as being more extreme in stereotyping. They saw boys as more alert, stronger, firmer, harder, and better coordinated than girls. A female's body and mind are thus believed to be trained differently from a male. Females are trained to "feel" rather than "act", to be captivating rather than to captivate (Johnson, 1965 as cited in Hetherington, 1972). Thus, Kaschak (1992) writes, "Every individual inhabits a body, and eventually habit sculpts its forms (p. 48)".

Few effects of paternal absence on the development of daughters have been found in the preschool or elementary school years. These effects, however, may only become apparent once these children experience puberty and begin to interact more frequently and consistently with males. In a study by Hetherington (1972), measuring the effects of father absence on personality development in adolescent daughters, it was found that the effects of father absence on daughters appear during adolescence and are evident most often as an inability to act appropriately in the presence of males. These effects were said to be particularly apparent in the non-verbal measures recorded with both a male and a female interviewer. With male interviewers, daughters of single-parent mother's showed proximity seeking and a more smiling, open and receptive manner than girls from intact or widowed families. Furthermore, these girls reported more dating and sexual intercourse early on in their lives.

Another study found that the absence of a father has been correlated with more aggression, school maladjustment, excessive sexual preoccupation and social acting out behaviours in females. A probable cause for these types of behaviours may be directly rooted in the frustration that may stem from a series of unsuccessful attempts to find a male figure with whom to establish a meaningful long-term relationship (Biller & Weiss, 1970).

Further implications have been made with regard to father-daughter relationships and long-term behaviour. It has been suggested that father-daughter relationships were associated with women's courtship patterns in college. Women who were involved in long-term romantic relationships with the intention to marry compared to those who were not, reported closer relationships with their fathers (Biller & Weiss, 1970).

Adolescence is often a time when parents view their children as coming-of-age; it is a rite of passage. Prior to this stage children are still viewed as innocent. Their socialization has allowed them to form relationships and friendships that are satisfying to them. Girls' desires and wishes are often expressed and responded to within their little groups and circles as well as by their families. As puberty hits, however, a transformation takes place;

differential treatment occurs with regards to how girls are treated both by their parents and by society in general (Gilligan, 1991).

Much of the literature spanning an entire century now have described adolescence as being a time when girls evidence adjustment difficulties. Girls at both end of the social class spectrum who are bright, intelligent, and sociable, find themselves in trouble during adolescence. Adolescence is a time that is marked by increased episodes of depression, eating disorders, poor body image, suicidal thoughts and gestures and a drop, in girls' sense of self-worth (Peterson, 1988).

Further studies have indicated that when families are stressed, with factors such as, marital conflict, economic hardship, or dismantling of the family, the children who are most psychologically at risk are boys in childhood and girls in adolescence (Elder & Caspi, 1990). Before puberty, girls are described as having a more positive outlook on life; aspirations and desires seem to be more within their grasp (Seligman 1975). They seem to have a better grasp on, and be able to handle and manage both their internal world, including their thoughts and their external world. However, with the onset of puberty, girls' outlook changes; and evidence of previous resiliency diminishes (Block, Block & Gjerde, 1986). Girls' attention appears to turn outward during this time; and they start to place value on things outside of themselves rather than their own internal values that once occupy all of their time and attention. This dramatic shift in girls' development from pre-puberty to puberty, may be one of the leading contributing factors to the large discrepancies in the rate of depression between men and women in adulthood, and not the experiences in childhood as many studies suggest (Seligman, 1975).

Girls' relational capacity prior to adolescence, such as their sense of freedom and expression of thoughts and feelings, become suppressed in adolescence (Gilligan, 1991). A team of more recent researchers investigating women's psychological development have shed some more light on the findings described above (Gilligan, 1991;

Kaplan & Klein, 1991; Miller, 1991; Surrey, 1991). These researchers have primarily focused on important aspects of women's psychological development, covering diverse topics, such as women and work, power, anger, incest, empathy and eating patterns, among others. The authors' proposed that there are important sex differences in the experience and construction of the self for both females and males (Gilligan, 1991; Kaplan & Klein, 1991; Miller, 1991; Surrey, 1991). A central theme that emerged from this theory is that, "women's sense of self becomes very much organized around being able to form and then maintain affiliation and relationships (p. 61)".

The underlying theme throughout much of this research is that, "self" in women may be experienced in a way that is not addressed by current psychoanalytic and developmental theories. The construction of the "Self-in-relation" theory is believed to have played an important part in understanding female development and has proved helpful in suggesting new and original programs and therapeutic interventions for supporting women (Gilligan, 1991; Kaplan & Klein, 1991; Miller, 1991; Surrey, 1991).

Traditional developmental theories continue to stress the importance of separation from the mother at early stages of childhood development, from the family at adolescence (Erikson, 1963), and from teachers and mentors in adulthood (Levinson, 1978) in order for the individual to form a distinct, separate identity. "High value is placed on autonomy, self-reliance, independence, self-actualization, "listening to and following" one's own unique dream, destiny, and fulfilment (p. 243), (Westkott, 1989)." The Self-in-relation theory, however, suggests that, for women, "a different - and relational - pathway is primary and continuous, although its centrality may have been "hidden" and unacknowledged (p. 24)" (Gilligan, 1991; Kaplan & Klein, 1991; Miller, 1991; Surrey, 1991).

The notion of the "Self-in-relation" to others denotes an important shift in emphasis from separation to relationship as the foundation for self-growth and development. Further, "relationship" is seen as the basic goal of development: that is, "deepening capacity for relationship and relational competence (p 124)." The self-in-relation model assumes that other aspects of self (such as, creativity, autonomy, assertion) develop within this primary context (Gilligan, 1991; Kaplan & Klein, 1991; Miller, 1991; Surrey, 1991). Hence, other aspects of self-development emerge in the context of relationship, with no intrinsic need to disconnect or to sacrifice relationship for self-development. This theory refers to relationship as involving an experience of "mutual empathy".

Both Kaschak (1992) and Hyde (1996) indicated that most women have a greater ability for relatedness, emotional closeness, and emotional flexibility than do most men. For boys, there is more of a preoccupation with early emotional separation and with forming an identity that is different or independent from others. Thus, promoting a relational attitude of dissociation and individuation. Girls on the other hand, develop the expectation that they can facilitate the growth of a sense of self through psychological connection and expect that the mutual sharing of experience will lead to psychological growth.

In traditional models as in Erikson's Developmental stages (Erikson, 1968) for example, after the first stage in which the aim is the development of basic trust; the aim of every other stage until young adulthood is some form of increased separation or self-development. The aim is not developing a greater capacity to form emotional connection with others; nor is it for contributing to an interchange between people; or for facilitating the growth of others as well as one's self. Nevertheless, when an individual arrives at the stage called "intimacy", they are expected to naturally be able to be intimate with another person even though they have spent all of their prior development striving for something very different (Westkott, 1989).

Borrowing from the self-in-relation theory, girls spend much of their development trying to identify with and relate to others;

whereas, boys strive for independence. Prior to adolescence, girls and boys are free and open to explore and express their own form of relating in the groups they form. However, adolescence usually marks a period of intense change, an extension of one self from their immediate and comfortable circles (Gilligan, 1991). Females seek out relationships in which they can achieve a mutual kind of relating and sharing while males seek out the kind of relating from which they are accustomed. Because both males and females have developed their own impressions, schemas and perceptions of self, relationships or relating from birth on, neither of them know how they should behave in each other's company. They both exhibit the characteristics or the stereotypical behaviours they have observed and/or were modeled for them but these are in opposition to each other. Females seek empathy in relationships where as men seek independence. Neither one is familiar or trained on how to be like the other or how to like one another.

Yet, another theoretical perspective is offered to explain how children develop psychologically throughout the lifespan. Children are said to learn primarily through imitation (Schroeder, 1992; Santrock, 1992; Landers, 1996, Myers, 1989). According to the social learning theory, children learn to imitate reinforcing and reinforced models in their environment. The pre-school child is said to rely on the primary role (consistently the mother/primary caregiver) model in his/her life for an understanding of what is deemed acceptable behaviour. It is believed that parents provide the appropriate role models that children use as a guide for past, present and future behaviours. Mothers, because of their primary nurturant role, tend to have strong influences on their child(ren)'s moral development and values. Specifically, the quality of mother-child relationship influences the child's understanding of another's feelings; that is, their development of empathy. This school of Developmentalists believe that the way that a mother responds to a distressing situation provides a model for the child's response in a similar situation (Myers, 1989; Santrock, 1992; Schroeder, 1992).

Interestingly, the traits and qualities that are most valued in society get expressed and reinforced while other traits are suppressed and unacknowledged. The traits of men are often seen as more valuable and are applauded and rewarded in society. On the other hand, women's traits are placed in subordination to those of men, are valued less and are often seen as weak. Women's desires are, therefore, suppressed, forcing them to adopt to a new script, a more masculine ideal. This turn of events according to the self-in-relation theory leads to inner conflict and a shutting down of women's voices and self-expression (Gilligan, 1991; Kaplan & Klein, 1991; Miller, 1991; Surrey, 1991).

I believe that both the traditional developmental models and the more recent self-in-relation model have merit and have contributed to the advancement of human development. Nevertheless, it is my belief that such models are continuously being used by popular media to perpetuate stereotypes of how men and women behave or should behave. For example, some of the traditional models, addressing human development, place their focus primarily on the external environmental events such as socialization or other externalizing behaviours to understand the nature of human development. Furthermore, some continue to focus on certain aspects of individuals (such as their gender) to explain the total individual. They tend to do this by studying the male model and, thus, generalizing the characteristics found to explain all of human behaviour.

The newer self-in-relation theorists, which constitutes only one aspect of feminist thought in this area, are offering an alternative point of view to human development. Nonetheless, they continue to feed the traditionally constructed female stereotypes of care, empathy, warmth and nurturance. Westkott (1989) writes, "I believe that this new paradigm inadvertently reproduces traits of care and empathy from the larger social contexts in which they are actually cultivated and these traits are idealized as normative for all human beings (p. 24S)." This according to Westkott, narrows the notion of female's "self-expression" and deepens the expectation that women should continue to "embrace relational empathetic behaviours (p. 245)" in order to form and maintain a sense self.

Consequently, neither model in my view have produced a clear and conclusive answer as to why humans behave the way they do but rather they simply explore what is unique to some males and females experience in the Western culture. Nevertheless, I did find other theoretical perspectives, which are presented below, which support my beliefs and theoretical perspective. Although the following perspectives have also been criticized for focusing on merely one aspect of an individual's development of self, that is, the focus on the internal, innate, self-actualizing force, disregarding the social aspects (Gleitman, 1991), they still came closest to my perspective of the self and include an important dimension neglected or dismissed by other theories which tend to focus solely on the external dimensions. Therefore, there is a need for consideration of both dimensions in attempting to describe the development of self. Taking my view of the universal self, Allport (1961), an author of the existentialist thought, writes this, "existentialism deepens the concepts that define human condition... and in so doing prepares the way for the first time for a psychology of human kind" (pp. 94-99).

Existential Psychology / Humanistic Psychology

Questions such as Who am I? What am I? What is my purpose? What is my relationship to others...and many more, have occupied the minds of human beings for as long as we have been in existence. Existentialist /Humanistic psychologists have sought the answers to such questions by looking within the individual through dynamic interactions and through a sharing of experiences. They believe that the answers to the meaning of human existence lie within human beings rather than within beautifully lined and painted walls within which animals are poked and prodded and studied to help explain human behaviour (Maslow, 1954; May, Allport, Feifel, Maslow & Rogers, 1961).

Both Humanistic and Existentialist psychologists hold the view that most other psychological theorists, be it psychodynamic or behaviourist, have lost sight of the true meaning of human nature. They believe that healthy humans strive for a sense of freedom to choose and make decisions about their existence rather than be led as puppets by some external force or drive or by an internal unconscious impulse. Both schools of thought hold the notion that humans want to strive, grow and realize their true potentials, to be the best they can be and therefore, to become self-actualized (May, Allport, Feifel, Maslow & Rogers, 1961).

Maslow (1954) thus, developed a hierarchy of needs which he viewed as a journey that all individuals go through in an attempt to reach the ultimate goal which he called "self-actualization". He asserted that people will only seek higher-order needs once the lower-order needs were met. Self-actualization or the self, in self-actualization is said to refer to one's "self-concept" and is developed in early childhood and eventually comes to include one's sense of oneself as a determiner who chooses to act or not act, make a decision or not make a decision. The self here is said to be concerned with subjective experience, with what the individual thinks and feels presently in the moment (Rogers, 1959; 1961).

Carl Rogers, in his clinical work, came to realize that an important element in an adult human's mental health is a strong sense of personal "self-worth". He believed that in order to achieve this a child needs "unconditional positive regard"- a sense of being accepted and loved without any conditions. Thus, given a reasonable sense of "self-worth" and fulfilment of the lower-level needs, an individual is equipped with and may be fueled by that internal drive to get to the very top of Maslow's hierarchy of needs which is to be self-actualized (Maslow, 1968, 1970;

Rogers, 1961). The focus of existentialist and humanistic thought according to May (1961) is centering upon the individual person; the emphasis is on the human being as he/she is emerging, becoming.

It is my belief that both humanistic and existentialist thought presents some compelling arguments to human nature and development. Their notion of humans as becoming or emerging toward self-actualization and as agents or determiners of their own actions and decisions, make their arguments particularly intriguing and fascinating. Nevertheless, their theories have been widely criticized particularly with regard to Maslow's definition of "self" and the prominent people with whom he chose to explain it. Maslow's definition of "self" is criticized as lacking measurability and observability. Humanistic psychologists adopt the notion that human beings want to feel free to choose and to decide their path and life journey rather than have that decision decided for them via unconscious impulses or external forces.

In response to the criticisms of these theories, the "self" and "self-concept" in both these schools of thought are one that emerges during early childhood, and can be likened to a state of being, a presence, if you will, that an individual comes to realize as their ability to choose; as they mature and grow and become independent from their parents and caregivers, they come to realize that they can choose and affect their own lives, and ultimately take ownership over their existence. Maslow is further criticized for using prominent people who were already self-actualized or successful to support his theory. Nevertheless, to become self-actualized does not mean that one has to become famous like Einstein or Eleanor Roosevelt or Thomas Jefferson. It merely means that one can be whatever they choose to be by choosing and deciding the life they want to have based on their values, drive and purpose.

Carl Roger's theory of the "need for unconditional positive regard" was also met with scrutiny because of the difficult nature of explaining later personality development when looking at early child rearing practices (Gleitman, 1991). This notion of unconditional positive regard, however, is one way of attaining self-actualization without the necessary lived experiences that all humans experience on their journey to the top. An unconditional positive regard will ignite the force within an individual, the drive and the motivation to strive and keep reaching for the top at an early age. The experiences that individuals encounter in the interim and along their journey will undoubtedly challenge what they learned previously and test their resolve. For example, if a child was given the reign to do as they please or were offered choices through their early development, they may be more apt to develop a positive sense of self. However, as this child grows and detaches from their parents, other life experiences may enter and cause them to lose confidence in that sense of self.

Kraft (1938), in A Psychology of Nothingness, also presents a notion of self that is quite fascinating. In his theory, he speaks of two selves which he calls, Existential experience and Idiosyncratic experience. An Existential experience, according to Kraft, is essential to humans and necessary for their authentic and healthy living. Kraft further notes that although every human being must have an Existential experience, each individual has a choice in the way they face them. An Idiosyncratic experience then, is said to be primarily a function of a person's personality, endowment, environment, history, expectations, values and attitudes. Therefore, an Idiosyncratic experience is said to be unique to everyone. Kraft notes that, "Unlike an Existential experience, it is neither essential for authentic living nor is it common to all humans (pp. 28-29)."

The main difference then between the Existential experience and Idiosyncratic experience is that an Existential experience is grounded in a person's personality structure as an essential "life-force". An Idiosyncratic experience on the other hand, is contingent on a person's unique life experiences and circumstances (socialization). Kraft (1938) asserts that an, "Existential experience is necessary for authentic living but an Idiosyncratic experience can either promote or impede authentic living (p.30)." For instance, an individual can view a negative life experience as defeating, damaging, a failure or as an opportunity to learn, grow and push on. One strives for authenticity and self-attainment while the other, due to their negative lived experiences and conditioning, cannot see the striving in the experience as they have fallen victim to their guilt, sorrow, blame and anger and uses this energy, rather than their authentic self, as their new impetus to push on.

Summary/Rationale

Having persevered through the review of family history, current family trends, traditional Developmental theories, the more recent self-in-relation theory, the social learning theory, and more prominently, the humanistic/existential perspectives, the reader might well ask, "How do all of these theories connect?" The common denominators, of course, are as follows: The development of self in daughters of single moms and their propensity to form and maintain intimate relationships with men. The review of the past and current empirical literature reveals considerable professional contributions to our clinical and scientific understanding of the development of human nature. However, few studies have investigated how being raised in a single parent (mother-headed) household affects the development of a daughter's sense of self as well as her ability to form and maintain an intimate relationship with a man.

Traditional Developmental theorists' have laid the framework for this discussion, viewing the absence of the male model in a female-only headed household as detrimental to a female child's social and psychological well-being especially during adolescence.

The following theoretical models and framework were selected because they best supported this thesis rationale. The Self-in-Relation model demonstrates how the differential treatment of girls and boys through socialization, contributes to the later difficulties that girls experience during adolescence. Similarly, the Social Learning theory was utilized because it represents strongly how children, through socialization, acquire later behavioural and emotional skills and their capacity to develop empathy. The Self-in-Relation theorists used this model of empathy development as one of their basic tenets for female development. Finally, existential and humanistic psychology were used because they came the closest in answering questions related to the development of self this author was seeking. Hence, the author contends that a myriad of factors go into developing an individual's sense of self, including the competing factors of their socialization (how society categorizes, frames and defines them based on socioeconomic class and family make-up) and their many lived experiences (actual experiences they have had along the way within and without the single parenting context and the choices they came to make as they journeyed through life), will ultimately determine their later social and psychological well-being and their capacity to move beyond socialization to ultimately attaining their true sense of Self and or becoming self-actualized.

Human beings grow and develop quite differently and uniquely revealing a diverse array of personalities; still, when surveying the general population, you will find that personalities span both ends of the human spectrum, with the most common personalities, hovering in the middle and forming the majority of the population, and the extremes or less common, hanging out on either end. Since single parent families make up a sub category of the larger population, their diversity can be likened to that of the general population. For instance, while some single parent family models develop "normally", thrive and are successful, others experience extreme adverse effects, struggle and face hardship upon hardship. Still, there is the group in the middle who share many commonalities and may evidence general life difficulties but have chosen to develop a variety of coping strategies, some of which may prove helpful, healthy, adaptive, and effective, while others prove less so, but they continue to hover in the middle. As the individuals in the middle struggle to understand and make sense of their reality, they may seek out help from friends, family members or professionals to assist them in coming to terms with their struggles. This study seeks to give voice to the daughters of single parent families by exploring some of the pathways in which they travel in their quest to find and make sense of their genuine and authentic self and their innocent attempts to establish and maintain intimate relationships with men. It further seeks to compare their development of self to the theoretical perspectives of the self, described above.

A qualitative research study was conducted which solicited data from the lived experiences of women about growing up in a single-mother household, their capacity to maintain intimate heterosexual relationships as well as their development of self from this context. It is the hope that the results of such an investigation would provide parents and society at large with knowledge about the many damaging effects that socialization can have on a child(ren)'s later development of self and thus their psychological well-being.

The objective of this investigation necessitates a qualitative measure because it is the only measure that allows a humanistic and open-ended approach to obtaining rich and actual experiences of live participants; and, because researchers continue to research single-parent families using quantifiable/measurable data, and their findings, time and time again present the single-parent family as a deficit model. They emphasize and propagate the negative stereotypes that have plagued single-parent families for decades. Furthermore, a search of the available research on daughters raised in a single-mother household, their development of self and capacity to maintain intimate relationships with men, did not produce any results. Instead, the focus of most of the studies was on childhood or adolescent experiences.

The impetus from which this quest or journey evolved came from my own personal lived experiences, as a daughter raised by a single mother, and my struggles with the choices I made navigating through life. It is my intention for this study to be explorative and perhaps influential in nature as its findings are original, interesting and thought provoking. This study will also contribute, additionally, to the current body of literature which tries to explain human growth and development. Hence forth, this study attempts to explore how the experiences of women raised by single mothers affect their development of self under the following conditions:

- The level of comfort and ease that females raised in single, mother-headed households have when forming and maintaining intimate relationships with men
- Participants' overall perceptions of being raised by a single mom.
- Whether the absence or limited exposure to a male, father-head model affected the way they approach intimate relationships with men.

- Whether their perceptions of being raised by a single mom contributed to their views on marriage.
- Whether participants viewed the absence or limited exposure to a father figure as affecting their views on trust in forming intimate relationships with men.
- Whether daughters from single parent homes saw themselves as more independent and self-reliant.

This thesis seeks to explore the development of self and the effects being raised by a single mother have on the ability of their daughters to form and maintain intimate relationships with men. The single parent family, mother-headed, is used as the backdrop or context within which this research is framed. An exploration of the literature on the family construct in the Canadian and American cultures as well as some psychological theories were used to explain a child's development throughout their life span. An illustration of the pervasiveness of human social perceptions in traditional research as well as their projections and influence on an individual's development is provided. These perceptions are formed based on what has been popularized by the media, thus becoming prescriptions for how we should behave. Furthermore, my own insights into human growth and development, which stems from the current data, as well as the exploration and consideration of some aspects of existential and humanistic psychology are presented herein.

Chapter 3

Methodology

Throughout my training in the field of psychology, I have learned a variety of ways in which to conduct and carry out psychological studies. For example, data is collected through a variety of means including the following: Questionnaires, surveys, pre-test - post-test, observation, field notes, focus groups, interviews, etcetera. My experience with both quantitative and qualitative methodological paradigms has led me to the conclusion that a qualitative method of approach was the most appropriate for this study (Rossman & Rallis, 1998; Denzin & Lincoln, 1994; Guba, 1990 & Wilson, 1977). My research focus and interests were related to how daughters raised by single mothers maintained intimate relationships with men as well as to their development of self. I listened to the voices of each participant, drawing conclusions from their own words. This, therefore, necessitated the need for a precise communication exchange using active engagement, careful listening, and intuitive probing in order to make sense and understand the participants' narratives. At times I struggled with this process because I was taught, in my undergraduate program, that I should be as objective in the process of research as possible. It was my perception and belief that the less interaction and the more robotic I could be, the more credible my results, and any interaction or interjections would contaminate the process.

As I reflect upon the writing and data gathering process of my undergraduate thesis, images of the room and participants came to mind. Participants filed into an empty classroom where I sat waiting for them to sign in; once there, I handed out questionnaires and ushered them to a desk, while I sat quietly at a desk in front of the room supervising the process and making sure that participants were not interacting with each other, for if they did, their questionnaires would be spoiled and would be of no use to me. The entire process was rigid and non-interactive; participants had to be very quiet as they filled out the questionnaires and exited the room. There was minimal interaction between myself and the participants, other than the usual description of the study and the ''thank you' that followed afterwards. Ann Oakley (1982) too, talks about her struggles between the traditional interviewing using a, "masculine paradigm" and the more recent "feminist interviews of women". She notes the interactive and valuable role that interviewers play throughout the interview process. She holds the belief that,

> the goal of finding out about people through interviewing is best achieved when the relationship of the interviewer and interviewee is non-hierarchal and when

the interviewer is prepared
to invest her own personal
identity in the relationship
(p. 41).

It is Oakley's perception that this will
facilitate a level of comfort and trust in
participants, thus allowing for a more natural
flow of telling and a more fullness and
richness of data. My interest in psychology
and more specifically of exploring the lives
of daughters of single parent families, their
development of self and capacity to maintain
intimate relationships with men, began many
years ago with my own struggles of making
sense of who I was as an individual and with
the world of people and things around me. As
a young child growing and evolving, I always
had a curious and inquisitive mind; and
today, very little has changed. I was always
in search of answers and ways of developing
myself further. When I started university in
my early twenties, I took courses that helped
me to make sense of myself. I began learning
about the construction of the family and

more specifically, the "nuclear family", its conception and popularization. Growing up under the umbrella of a single parent family, I quickly came to learn that this type of family make-up was not valued by society at large and as a matter of fact, was often viewed as "abnormal". The majority of the literature that I read pertaining to the single parent family, portrayed it as dysfunctional and children raised in such a family were often rated as less likely to succeed as children and adults. The popular and prevailing research presents single parent families as substandard or subservient; they are described as not measuring up to the more acceptable two-parent family. Hence, the government continues to endorse the notion of the nuclear family and writes policies which advocate that single parent families are broken and are thus considered a "deficit model" of family.

The notion that my family construct was not valuable and seen as "abnormal" by popular media, affected me greatly, my state of being, and my citizenship to Canada. I began to feel ashamed of the family with whom I was raised. I conjured up excuses upon excuses as to why my father was not a part of my life or why I was not in contact with him. The feelings that these types of questioning evoked, resulted both in anger and a need to understand my anger; a need to understand why I was feeling ashamed of who I am. My university training and experience allowed me to search for deeper meanings and understandings. It fostered an environment in which I could explore, find my voice and pursue original thinking. I developed an impetus to find a way of representing the single-parent family model in a positive light. I wanted to emphasize the good side, the strengths, if you will, of single parent families. I believe that my mother is one of the strongest human beings on this planet. She has done an outstanding job raising me on her own. She showered me with her unconditional love and adoration daily which I now wish to share with others. She is my hero in every way and it would be wrong for the world to think of her as anything less than that.

Therefore, my curiosity and passion for conducting this research came simply from being the product of a single mother and the need to represent this type of family construct in a positive manner. To conduct such a study requires one to elicit some very personal and private experiences of someone's life. The level, quality, and amount of telling will vary from person to person, thus one may likely end up with mounds of knowledge and data with which to make sense of. Selecting the mode of inquiry that will provide as close an approximation of the story tellers' experiences is of tremendous importance. A variety of paradigms that fall under the structure of qualitative research exist; such as, ethnography, phenomenological, case study, focus groups, participant-observer, and others (Rossman & Rallis, 998). Nevertheless, I chose the grounded theory theoretical framework to allow the data to determine which root it would travel. Strauss and Corbin (1990, 1997), demonstrate how grounded theory is, "inductively derived from the study of the phenomenon it represents" (in this case, daughters of single parent families, their development of self and maintenance of interpersonal relationships with men). According to Strauss and Corbin (1990), grounded theory is, "discovered, developed, and provisionally verified through systematic data collection and analysis of data pertaining to the phenomenon (p. 23)" under investigation. There is an ongoing interplay between the data collection, analysis and theory. One does not begin with a theory then prove it, but rather, one begins with an area of study and allows what is relevant from the study to emerge.

Asking one to reflect on their lived experiences on such a personal topic can be both a cathartic and reflective process which can conjure up perceptions of experiences already passed. It is my belief that the study's participants demonstrated a richness of lived experiences and thus, perceptions, which they have chosen to share with me. These experiences, I suspect, have more than likely contributed to their development of self and their ability to maintain intimate relationships with men.

Participants

Participants were obtained via what is termed, the snow ball effect, which began with one participant volunteering for the study and then tendering names of other potential participants. Participants were informed of my status as the daughter of a single mother and was provided with an overview of the thesis topic. It is my belief that because I shared a similar social terrain as these participants, trust and level of comfort were almost immediately realized. Even though I did begin the process with a specific psychological construct such as self, I attempted to be as non-directive as possible, using an open-ended interview format. Therefore, allowing the participants to determine the procedure as much as possible.

Participants consisted of six women who were raised by a single mother; four of the women were within the 25 -35 age group and two were within the 18 -24 age group. All participants had post-secondary education and training. Two were first year university students, one had a bachelor's degree, plus a college certificate, and three had graduate degrees. Four of the participants came from varying professions. Two were teachers, one a teacher assistant and the other was seeking employment in the mathematics field. Participants were selected through personal contact. This study's participants and professional colleagues also tendered names of potential participants. The geographic locations from which the participants were selected also varied. Three of the participants lived on Prince Edward Island and three lived in the Halifax area. One participant moved to Prince Edward Island from Ontario, Canada.

Participants came from varying backgrounds but all were raised by a single mother at some point during their lives. At least four of the participants were aware of who their fathers were and had contact with them. Three participants lived with both parents in the same house for a period of time. One participant lived with both parents for the first two years of her life; another for the first seven years; and still another for the first 13 years. One participant never lived with both parents in the same house but had ongoing contact with her father for a number of years, such as weekends, summer holidays, Christmas, etc. One participant lived with her mother only until she was 15 years old and another participant lived only with her mother.

Three of the participants gained a stepfather when they were teenagers. Their mothers marry or re-married when they were approximately 15 years old. One of the participants lived with her stepfather for two years, from 15 to 17 years of age and the other two participants lived in the same house with their mother and stepparent.

Participants also varied in family make-up. At least three of the participants were only children; two participants had three siblings; and the other had one sibling.

Family dynamic was also different. At least two participants were raised as part of an extended family unit, whereas the other four relied mostly on the immediate family for support (i.e., their mothers).

There was no focus on wider issues of class which may have significantly impacted on the level of self in relationships.

Materials

Materials consisted of a list of 28 interview questions concerning background information on each participant, dating history, as well as the socialization of gender roles. This set of questions were developed by the author to elicit participants' perceptions/experiences of being raised by a single mother; to explore varying themes pertaining to the development of interpersonal intimate relationships with men and its maintenance, as well as their development of self. Also, a cassette tape recorder and eight cassettes were used for recording and data gathering.

Procedure

The gathering of data from interviews involved the social construction of knowledge. Therefore, the participants' rendition of their lived experiences and development of self at the time of the interview, may only be relevant to that moment in time. If the interviews were to be conducted two months previously or two months later, their stories may be very different from the ones described in this study.

Each participant was interviewed individually. Interview locations varied, however, all participants were interviewed in a quiet room with minimal distractions (when possible). Most interviews were conducted at the participants' homes. Some were at their offices and one was at the researcher's home. These locations were agreed upon prior to the interview by both the researcher and the interviewee. The tape recorder was placed at a reasonably close distance to both the participant and the researcher to ensure an audible transmission of information.

Prior to the actual interview, the participants were asked to sign a variety of documents, including the following: A consent form for participating in the study and for the recording of the interview, and a release of information form regarding content and its potential inclusion in this study's publication. Participants were also verbally informed of measures undertaken in this study to protect confidentiality. Each participant was also informed that she could withdraw from the study at any time without suffering any adverse consequences.

A quasi-clinical, semi-structured, interview technique was employed. This design consisted of the investigator presenting the participants with a set of 28 specific questions with a series of "free inquiries". Moreover, in addition to the standard questions, the researcher sought elaboration on certain responses for further clarification as well as pursued idiosyncratic or anecdotal information. Interview questions were both open ended in style, to gather general information, and, specific, in order to elicit answers to this study's questions.

Analysis

The body of experiences that this study elicits, were analyzed using the grounded theory approach to qualitative research. This approach requires a researcher to allow the relevant information to grow out of the data which pertains to the topic under investigation. This approach is rooted in the philosophy that themes and patterns from across all individuals will emerge and present itself to the researcher. Themes from this study were chosen by the researcher upon analysis of the data; that is not to say that other themes did not emerge. Similarly, it is my perception that had the data been read by other parties, other themes may have been noted. Based on the researchers' area of inquiry, the data was examined and responses were grouped together according to the same or similar responses pertaining to a particular topic. The groupings were then further broken down into main categories and labelled as such; for instance, relationship to mother, would represent one category or theme. The grounded theory approach necessitates the author to move beyond the individual narratives, and interpretations of the narratives as presented by the participants, to gain greater insights and understanding of a mother-headed, single-parent household. For instance, the relationships between mother and daughter, as well as the struggles, triumphs and later outcomes were also examined.

The individual interviews were transcribed and the transcripts reviewed by both the researcher as well as the respondents (when possible). The respondents reviewed the transcripts to check for accurate representation and in some cases provided further clarification of ideas and meanings or embellishment of thoughts. Consistencies and discrepancies were also noted, reported and described.

Ethical Considerations

Although the participants' involvement in this study was entirely voluntary, it was the responsibility of the researcher to ensure that their well-being remained intact during and after the study. The author ensured that the participants' understood the meaning of informed consent by verbally asking them after they read the consent forms. Participants' determined the level of disclosure beginning with the use of either their own name or pseudonyms. The nature as well as the participants' involvement in the study were explained prior to the actual interview. Furthermore, participants were advised that any information they provided was entirely at their discretion. Due to the personal nature of this process, participants were debriefed and where applicable, a list of counselling resources were provided to participants who felt they needed to continue with this unleashing of such personal and private information as well as the feelings it evoked in them.

Chapter 4

Results

The findings of this study are reported in this chapter. Upon analysis of the six interview transcripts, six themes emerged. These themes presented themselves after careful and in-depth study of the data. Each question from the list of interview questions were analyzed individually at first. They were then grouped into categories based on recurring themes or similarities in answers from the participants. The six themes that emerged included the following: **relationship with men, trust, modelling, relationship with mother, marriage and self-reliance/independence**. The overall themes that this study sought to make sense of were of a daughters' capacity to maintain intimate relationships with men, their development of a sense of self in the context of being raised by a single mom, as well as through a variety of lived experiences. The themes are described below as are the voices and experiences of the women in this study.

Relationship with Men

Five of the six women reported being comfortable in the company of men with whom they were not trying to establish or maintain an intimate relationship. They indicated that professionally and socially they were comfortable with mingling and having male friends but intimacy with men was more difficult. One participant who reported not feeling comfortable with men, described her experience as such, when asked, "How comfortable do you feel in the company of men?" Her response was, *"everything about it makes me uncomfortable."* Nevertheless, all of the women reported having varying numbers and length of time in intimate relationships. Some never had an intimate relationship while others had many relationships. Factors such as participant's age may account for some variation in number of relationships.

The most significant and meaningful relationships as indicated by each of five participants, are described in this section. Alice, 31 years old, describes her first significant relationship as one in which her partner at the time, "*had a lot of baggage.*" She said she thought she, "could change him". However, he became "*very abusive*" towards her, "*verbally and emotionally at first and then it became physical.*" She said she was, "*very afraid and felt lost in an abusive relationship.*" She noted that she "*...cut herself off from her friends and didn't like herself at all.*" She said she questioned what it was about her that made her get involved with someone who did this to her. She eventually got out of the relationship and pressed charges. The relationship lasted for about one year.

Alice further noted that she is not comfortable showing emotions in a relationship. She remarks that, "*I will never show them how I feel...l would feel it but I would never let them know...l have no idea how they would know how I feel...I just think they know."*

Martha, 25 years old, indicated that she went on her first date when she was *"22 years old."* However, she says she, *"...has never been out with someone that she was actually interested in."* *"They just asked"*, she said, *"and I went out."* She notes that she never initiates contact after a date; she waits for them to call her. If someone did call, she said, *"I didn't mind talking...but I wouldn't call them."* Martha also indicated that she has never felt comfortable talking about her feelings and she would often tell men who showed an interest that she is only interested in *"being friends."* She notes that she, *"can't imagine herself in a relationship, but could really easily imagine herself being a single parent."* She says, *"I could imagine myself looking after children and cooking...I can visualize all that...but I can't imagine what it would be like to be in a relationship and sometimes that scares me."*

Melissa, 33 years old, describes her experiences in relationships as being, *"really intense very quickly.*" She notes that when she gets into a relationship with someone she really likes, she,

> *"Jumps in with two feet and away she goes ...and I'm gaga in love...and I want to spend all of my time with this person and really be nurturing and caring with this person... Friends, when I was younger, took less importance to my boyfriends."*

Melissa's first significant relationship started in university near the end of her second year. They met in one of her classes and became friends. She stresses this point because she said that most of the other men she was dating at the time, she, *"met in bars and just started a relationship with them."* This guy, I'll call James, was *"special"*. Melissa notes, *"it was the most significant relationship because it was the one that allowed me to be the most vulnerable, to trust and believe what he said.*" She further indicated that she enjoyed the fact that she knew James "*respected*" her, what she was doing, and her thoughts and ideas. She said, "*he respected me as a person and that meant so much to me.*" The relationship lasted two and half years. James ended the relationship because he had an affair. They got back together but the "*level of trust*", Melissa notes, had changed and things were never the same. James ended the relationship a second time. Melissa said she was "*devastated even though I saw it coming*" because she thought this was the person for her. She further stated this relationship and its ending, "*set me back for years…in terms of who I am and what I was about and my self-worth.*" She said that it has taken her almost "*10 years*" to get over it because she had also become very close to his family.

Jamie, 26 years old, met the boy she went on her first date with in grade one. They knew each other throughout their schooling and she described their initial relationship as being "*buddies*". They began dating in grade 10 and she described the relationship as being really close. They became members of each other's families; and they shared the same circle of friends. Jamie describes the relationship as both of them "*bringing out the best in each other.*" She said, "*I would be spending the rest of my life with him.*" I'll call him Brad, but this was not the case. The relationship lasted six years and Brad ended it. Jamie said he told her that he "*didn't love her anymore.*" She said she was "*really hurt*" because she was "*oblivious*" to it. She never saw it coming. "*It was really hard*", she notes.

Victoria, 19 years old, met her first "*true love*" in grade 10 and they dated for "*a year and a half.*" The relationship ended because she moved away to a foreign country as an exchange student. They tried to continue the relationship in the interim but her partner found it "*too difficult.*" She notes, "*I really loved him*" and would have loved to remain or maintain the relationship if she could.

Samantha, 19 years old, has never had an intimate relationship. She reports being "*gay*" but has never had a relationship, gay or otherwise. She said she was asked out by two boys in grades 11 and 12 but said "*no*" to them. She describes these two experiences as being "*upsetting*" because she said she waited all of those years to be asked out and it "*never happened.*" She would really like to meet someone but she does not like "*big crowds.*" She notes that she has a "*big fear*", that when she meets someone "*special*" she "*will not know what to do and may end up making a fool of herself.*"

Overall, all of the women reported having a wide variety of experiences with intimate relationships. The "older" participants had many more experiences to draw upon. The younger participants had less experiences to draw from and one of them had never experienced an intimate relationship; still, they both appeared to be trying to make sense of either past relationships or potential relationships as the interview unraveled.

Trust

All participants reported having some difficulty with trust in relationships whether it be intimate or otherwise. Most participants felt that trusting someone meant that they would be *"opening"* themselves up and rendering themselves *"vulnerable"* to *"hurt and pain."* Two participants felt that they were not *"worthy"* or *"loveable enough"* and said, *"perhaps that is why their fathers left their mothers and them."* They felt abandoned and have thus developed a *"fear of abandonment in relationships."* They indicated that they *"do not trust their partners to stick around and fear they will leave them."* Both participants reported actively seeking to end relationships before their partners ended it; thus, becoming a self-fulfilling prophecy.

Jamie noted that she had a *"fear of losing her mother."* As a teenager she says she *"remembers feeling a sense of mom, don't leave."* She notes, *"I was always fearful of my mother dying because she was such an important part of my life... There was just that sense of security that she was always going to be there."* She also noted trust issues pertaining to her father. She said that she *"...hopes when she marries, things will turn out differently for her than it did her mom and hopes that her mate does not turn out like her dad."*

Modelling

Three of the participants in the 25-35 age group perceived not having a consistent male-model in their lives as contributing in some way to their difficulty in maintaining an intimate relationship with men as well as with the development of a global sense of self. They felt that seeing their mother or parents interact in an intimate relationship, in terms of affection, sharing of thoughts and ideas, the resolution of disagreements, give and take, and what happened afterwards, would have prepared them to be more at ease and comfortable in similar situations.

Alice notes that,

> *"...a sense of what a man is supposed to do and what their role is and how they treat people by being around people so then in turn...l should be*

able to make that connection in terms of having seen this."

She further describes being in a relationship as this,

"it's like throwing me a basketball and I've never seen a basketball game before, so I don't know if I should bounce this ball, kick this ball, throw it or put it on my head...I don't know what to do with it."

Martha said her mother just started dating someone about a year ago after many years of being alone; she is hoping that she could, *"'watch this new relationship and learn from it because she wouldn't like to have the kind of relationship that her mom had with her father."* Finally, Melissa said *"...I didn't have any role models with a male that I would be publicly showing affection to...so I had a hard time with showing affection in public."* Most of these women felt a sense of *"uncertainty"* as to what to do as well as what to *"expect"* in a relationship.

The other half of the women did not feel it was necessary to have a male role model. Two of them felt that living with a single mom was all they ever knew and so it is difficult to imagine it any other way. One woman noted that she did not think that a child needed to have two parents. If the parent was *"'good"* and had *"good support"* then that would be okay. She said, *"look at me, I turned out just fine."* One of the other women thought that it would be worse to remain in a bad situation with two parents and be exposed to that all the time than being raised by a single mom.

Relationship with Mother

Four of the six participants reported having a sense of admiration for their mothers. They described their relationship as being very close and special. They all described their relationship with their mothers as being more of a friendship than a mother - daughter relationship. Alice said this about her relationship with her mother, *"...a very good relationship, real close...we talk quite often, very supportive, very encouraging and kind. She has a warm sense of humor...l love talking to her... telling her what 's going on in my life."* At least two of the participants who were closer in age to their mothers, described their relationship as being more like "sisters". Jamie said this about her relationship with her mother,

> *"...like with my mother, it's like a sister...l can't imagine a life without my mother...I was raised by a fantastic mother and have no question that she worked hard...and instilled in me that we had responsibilities...so I think she was a real model."*

She went on to say that, *"I admire her and love her dearly and I am proud of her...l think she is the person that I would like to be like and am in many ways...she is pretty special."* Melissa notes that she and her mother *"struggle between being friends and mother -daughter."* She notes that they are *"very close... she relies on me a lot and I rely on her."* Melissa describes her relationship with her mom as being *"very strong"*. She said *"I was really a shy kid so I clung to her a lot and our relationship was such from being a child up until now, that even when we are in a family gathering or something like that, we would be holding hands."*

The two youngest participants who were further apart in age with their mothers, perceived their relationship with their mothers as being more hierarchal. They described the relationship with their mothers as being more of a care-giver role, someone who provided financial and emotional support as well as perhaps discipline, rather than as a friendship or a sister role. Victoria describes her relationship with her mother as such,

> *"I think when I was younger especially because when you're a kid you have to rely on your parents more...you have to*

look to them for everything and you count on them more... you're less of a person than you are now...So when you're younger, your parents' way is the way of the world but then you grow up, you're like, hey, I don't agree with everything they say...so conflict... things aren't peachy...but I try and sort of respect that."

Victoria further notes *"...my mother has given me everything I have...She has given me life and she brought me up and she is paying for my university/education."*

All participants recognized and acknowledged the struggles and sacrifices that their mothers made for them throughout their upbringing. At least three participants stated that *"their mothers sacrificed their whole lives to make them who they are today."* One participant noted that she *"is very proud"* of her mother and she also said that her mother is *"the person she would like to be like."* Three participants indicated that their mothers went on social assistance so she could be at home to take care of them and spend as much time with them as possible. One participant notes, "*she wanted to stay at home when I was a kid between the ages of 1 and 3...she felt it was very important because she was from a large family and wasn't close to her parents.*" Two other participants indicated having the support of an extended family which they felt really helped their mothers in terms of babysitting and with providing them with extra love, care and attention. Jamie indicated that she felt "*really fortunate...I know I was really fortunate*" she said "*because of the extended family that I had...both my mother's side and my father's side of the family were working together at all times.*" Alice also noted that she was "*very close*" to her grandfather and great grandmother; they provided strong emotional support for both herself and her mother.

For the majority of the participants, it was difficult to comment on the advantages and disadvantages of being raised by a single mom because most said, "*they've only seen one model and couldn't comment on what they haven't been exposed to.*" Perhaps the one drawback many felt was the fact that they were not exposed to that interpersonal relating between men and women. For example, Melissa noted that "*there had been absolutely no man on the scene...I had no exposure to what my mother was like in a dating situation.*" On the other hand, one participant mentioned that it was "*advantageous*" to not see her parents "*fighting*" or "*squabbling*" all the time because that might have "*made matters worse.*"

Marriage

Four of the six participants said they have thought about and considered marriage. Three of the participants felt strongly about marriage and saw it as something that was important to them. One participant, although having thought about marriage, saw it as being "pointless" because in the end she noted that, "*if you love someone, you don't need a silly bunch of vows on a piece of paper to prove it.*" Also, due to the ending of her parent's marriage and a personal relationship, she said that she has come to believe that "*love ends*". The three participants who saw marriage as being important to them also equated it with raising a family. They felt strongly about having two parents present when raising children. They could not see themselves doing it alone like their mothers' did. One participant said this,

> *"although I do say one parent is fine, I always want to have another parent with me...I want to have children and I want my mate to help me raise those children...because I don't know if I could have done as good a job as my mother... things are also changing too."*

Two participants perceived marriage as being less important. One of them noted that in her observation the people she grew up around, "*getting married was something they did when their kids reached a certain age because it's more convenient after that point."* She went on to say that, *"...in terms of marriage being in a permanent relationship and being sort of the way you're supposed to be in society,"* she felt was *"intimidating"* or *"alien"*. All of the three participants who perceived marriage in a less favourable light, said they saw a, *"long term mutual agreement between two people"* as being *a more viable option to marriage."*

Self-Reliance and Independence

Self-reliance, though not an initial focus of this study, did surface as a sixth theme. All of the women demonstrated that with regards to achievement, they were not afraid to tackle areas of interests and set goals which they later accomplished. All of the women reported being very ambitious, seeing education as both important and valuable to their sense of self. Alice noted that, *"going to school and learning makes me feel very good about myself...It gives me a sense of esteem and confidence that no one could take away from me."* In addition, all of the women described themselves as being independent. They stressed how important it was to do things on their own. At least three of the participants indicated that they felt *"very uncomfortable"* asking others for help. They stated that they preferred to do things on their own, only eliciting help from others when *"absolutely necessary"*.

Overall, it appears that the daughters of single mothers in this study have a wide variety of lived experiences from which to draw. All of the women reported having difficulty with intimate relationships. Similarly, all of the women indicated that trust was difficult for them in relationships. They said it was not easy for them to trust someone for fear of hurt or disappointment. At least half of the women reported that they felt it was important to have a model of an intimate relationship from which they could watch and learn. The other half did not feel it was necessary. Four out of the six women reported having a close relationship with their mothers while the remaining two, the two youngest, felt the relationship was more hierarchal or unequal. At least four of the women felt that marriage was important; however, three of them equated it to having a family. The remaining three did not perceive the formal act of marriage to be necessary, but felt that a mutual agreement would suffice. Finally, all of the women reported being self-reliant and independent, seeing themselves as capable of doing whatever they wished without eliciting help from others.

The development of self, therefore, is interwoven between all of the above listed variables as well as the ones not listed and studied. It is not reliant on one variable or the other but rather, work in concert with all variables. The participants' lived experiences pertaining to those described above, and other overlapping experiences, have contributed to the way they have come to perceive intimate relationships, trust, modelling, relationship to mother, marriage, and self-reliance.

Chapter 5

Discussion

The purpose of this study was to explore the development of self and the ability of women, raised in a single parent, mother only household, to form and maintain intimate relationships with men. This study also sought to give a voice to six women who were brave enough to share their most intimate of experiences with me. A variety of experiences pertaining to the development of self and relationships were evidenced. The findings are discussed in this chapter and conclusions are drawn based on my personal insights and from related research studies. Implications are also offered both for additional studies in this area as well as for a critique of some of the related literature pertaining to this area of study.

Six semi-structured interviews, averaging an hour and a half in length, were conducted. The interviews followed a prepared outline of topic areas to be explored (Appendix A). Each interview was tape recorded and transcribed. Each transcript was read systematically and then categorized. Six themes emerged from the data. They are as follows:

1. The level of comfort and ease that daughters of single-parent families have when forming and maintaining intimate relationships with men.
2. The ability to build trust in intimate relationships with men.
3. The need, or a lack there of, for the modelling of intimate relationships with men for later comfort and referencing.
4. The overall perceptions of daughters raised by a single mother.
5. The need or importance of marriage for daughter's raised by single moms.

6.   Self-reliance and independence

Research Findings

First, I believe it is important to state, based on the data contained in this study and other related studies, that every single parent family situation is uniquely different. Similarly, every child born to a single mother is uniquely different; some may be born to financially rich parents, some from poor parents, some from average parents, some from violent parents, some from extremely negative or extremely positive parents, some from very loving and nurturing parents. There are no two experiences that are exactly the same. Every child born to a single mother will have a different life experience and experience different life struggles and triumphs along the way. Every child will form their own sets of schemas, impressions and have their own perceptions based on their own unique lived experiences and every child will choose to maintain or discard schemas, impressions and perceptions that they gather along the way.

The findings of this study, thus, reflect the lived experiences as well as the learned schemas, impressions, perceptions and choices of the six women interviewed; as well as their journey to developing a sense of self.

Trust, and the capacity to form, maintain and share in intimate relationships with men are variables not found in other studies with regards to daughters of single mothers. This study found that all participants had a fear of trust in relationships. Two participants described it as a fear of abandonment and equated this fear to their father leaving and abandoning their family. They felt they were not "good enough" or "loveable enough" for him to stay. Three other participants noted that trusting someone is like opening themselves up to hurt and pain. Thus, they did not feel comfortable doing that. The last participant noted that she had a fear of her mother leaving. She notes that she was always afraid that her mother would die. She said she relied on her mother for everything. *"She was always there"*, she said, *"and so I just could not ever imagine her not being there"*. The same participant also hopes that her partner would not do what her father did, leaving both herself and her mother.

Most of the women had varying amounts and duration of experiences of intimate relationships with men. Some reported no encounters, some reported one, and others reported several. Similarly, their relationships lasted anywhere from one month to six years. Naturally, the experiences of participants aged 26 and older, appeared to have had a richness of experiences fully equipped with substantial details of trials and tribulations with intimate relationships, compared to their younger age counterparts. The most significant relationships as identified by the respondents were reported. Each participant had a very different experience regarding intimate relationships with men.

All participants had a sense of wanting a stable long-term relationship. However, circumstances dictated whether or not that were possible. For at least three of the participants their partners ended the relationship. Another participant ended the relationship because it was an abusive situation. One participant never had a relationship and still another just did not know how to be in relationships. Although lack of comfort with men, trust, modelling, and relationship to mother are all variables that the participants in this study used to describe as contributing to their sense of self or their struggles with developing a sense of self, other factors (such as, quality of relationships, siblings, extended family, etcetera) not investigated by this study, are all contributing factors.

The Social Learning theory states that children are likely to imitate what they see others do; thus, the six women may have gained other experiences from their parents, siblings and or relatives, that this study did not look at. Moreover, all of the lived experiences that one encounters contribute to the development of their sense of self as well as their ability to develop and maintain relationships intimate or otherwise. One's development of self, therefore, cannot be equated to one thing or another and in this case, being raised by a single parent. Therefore, in order to understand an individual's behavior and actions it is crucial that one takes a closer look at specific occurrences in an individual's life that may be contributing to why they behave the way they do rather than globally attributing their behavior to their parenting circumstance or experience.

For instance, each of the women may have had other factors in their lives that allowed them to perceive relationships as being one way or another. The commonality between all of the women of course, is being raised by a single mother. Nevertheless, the extent and quality of that relationship may have contributed to some of their perceptions. Some participants reported having ongoing contact with their fathers. Others reported having some; and still others reported having none. Some never knew their fathers at all. Having support or not from extended family members may also be a contributing factor for these women's perceptions of intimate relationships and with their development of self.

Some studies report that the absence of modeling for both single parents as well as their children, contributes to emotional issues and a sense of uncertainty as to what is appropriate and not appropriate (Morrison, 1995; Amato, 1995; Bandura, 1977; Guidubali, Perry & Natasi, 1985; Biller & Bahm, 1971; Amato, 1991; Mott, Kowaleski- Jone, Menaghan, 1991, Santrock, 1970; Lynn & Sawrey, 1959). The findings of the present study are consistent with the literature. Half of the participants in this study reported that not having a model to draw from made it difficult for them to be in intimate relationships. They noted that it is like doing something that they have no prior knowledge of and, therefore, they have no idea whether they are doing the right thing or not. The same participant who mentioned that she knew how to be a single parent because that was modelled for her, also noted that she has, "*no clue how to be in a relationship*". That, she says, "*is completely foreign to her*" and that "*scares*" her. Since her mother just recently started a relationship after many years of being alone, this participant hopes that she could watch her mother and learn from her how to be in a relationship. The other half of the participants did not think it was necessary to have a model. They noted that being raised by a single mother is the only thing they have ever known or remembered and therefore cannot imagine it any other way. A couple of the women indicated that if they moved from a two-parent home to a single-parent home perhaps they would be able to compare the two but, as it stands, they could not. One participant indicated that she did not think having a model was important because it would be like conforming to a way of doing things and she would rather learn to do it her own way.

From the participants' descriptions, all of their mothers appeared to have been committed to their daughters. Three participants reported that their mothers went on social assistance in order to be there for them and spend more time with them. Two participants noted that their mothers reached out to and received an abundance of support from their extended family members in order to provide more love and nurturance for them. The last participant noted that her mother provided her with life and have been very committed to her growth and development by exposing her to the richness of her culture either through travel and/or education. She is at a stage in her life, she notes, where she is dependent on her mother who has always been there for her.

Half of the women from this study saw marriage as positive and important for raising children. All three of them saw themselves as getting married and raising a family. Their perception was that they did not want to do what their mothers did because it was either too self-sacrificing or too difficult especially "*nowadays*". The other half of the women did not see marriage as necessary but viewed a mutual agreement between two people as a more viable option to marriage. One participant did have a child out of wedlock and is raising her child alone. Another participant indicated that she knew all that it takes to be a single mom because she has seen it. She notes that she knows how to take care of the family, prepare meals, listen to complaints or what have you. She further indicated that she has lived it and knows what is involved and what it takes. Hence, she says, *"I could easily see myself becoming a single parent because it is familiar to me."* Is it her perception then and her choice to say that she could see herself becoming a single parent based on what is familiar to her and her lived experiences or is it because she was raised by a single parent or both?

Although the majority of participants, except for one, reported that their mothers did not have university or post-secondary education and training early on in their development, all participants in this study had some post-secondary education and training and at least three had graduate degrees. Nevertheless, is it the result of being raised in a single-parent home to also have high educational attainment or is it the encounters, influences, experiences, their internal drive or a combination of all of these variables that allow them to perceive education as more or less important? The participants' in this study may have learned along the way that education is a valuable thing and hence developed a schema that allowed them to view education as a valuable experience, or the topic of study may have awakened an inner interest that pushed them on their educational path. Therefore, are their views of education attributed to being raised by a single mom and a desire to be more or is it their positive perception of education that allowed them to succeed or is it an internal, innate drive to do and be more, achieve to their highest potential in an area of interest, or is it all of those?

Four of the six participants were professionals or had professional degrees and two were university students; consequently, they all appeared to have somewhat of a comfortable lifestyle, enjoying the benefits of their hard work (education) or working towards their goals. None of the women studied reported being dependent on the welfare system or social assistance and none of them reported being divorced.

Contrary to popular beliefs, there were no evidence of psychiatric disturbances in any of the participants and none were reported. However, two participants did mention seeing a therapist and others had taken courses or were reading self-help books to work on dealing with interpersonal relations and their ongoing journey of their development of a sense of self.

It is interesting to note, that all of the women in this study described themselves as hard working and independent. They all appeared to strive for a sense of self in an area in which they could control (achievement/education). For example, education was important to all of the women and most saw it as providing a sense of confidence and esteem. All of the women were firm in their desire to accomplish things on their own without eliciting the help from others, that is, unless it was absolutely necessary. There was no fear of accomplishing or trying anything; anything was possible for these women. Their resilience and hard work certainly paid off for many of the women with regard to their achievement. All four of the working women reported enjoying what they do.

Although most of these women appeared to have an excellent sense of self regarding their achievement and education, their sense of self, as it pertains to intimate relationships with men, was quite the contrary. They seem to perceive having an intimate interpersonal relationship with a man as being more strongly linked to their sense of self, to who they are, than their educational attainment. Therefore, their sense of self in intimate relationships appeared to override their sense of self in other areas of achievement. One participant noted that if she could wish for anything it would be to have a family. At the same time, she indicated that her sense of esteem and confidence surface more when she is learning (i.e., education).

This finding is in accordance with the self-in-relation theory which states that there are important sex differences in the experience and construction of the self for both females and males. A central theme from this theory is that, "women's sense of self becomes very much organized around being able to make and then maintain affiliation in relationships" (Gilligan, 1991, Kaplan & Klein, 1991, Baker Miller, 1991 & Surrey, 1991). Hence, this theory is based on the notion that women must be in relationship with another in order to achieve a sense of self. The perceptions of the women being studied here appear to fit with this notion. One participant even mentioned that, *"it is expected of you once you reach a certain age to have someone in your life... and if you tell someone you meet that you don't have one then they look at you very strangely as if to say what is wrong with you."*

Self, for many of these women seem to be primarily based on external and environmental factors. The many variables described above which explains how the women of this study viewed and tried to make sense of the world of relationships, and their journey to finding a sense of self, support the notion that socialization and, thus, the perceptions gained through socialization and environmental influences contribute largely to their development of a sense of self and who they are. These women, therefore, appear to be the victims of the stereotypes that are perpetuated by society as noted in traditional and the more recent self-in-relation developmental theories.

Conclusions

As society changes, it appears that psychology changes along with it. During the hunting-gathering years, family functioned more as a unit which depended on its members to find creative ways of obtaining and providing food, clothing and shelter. They relied more on their instincts, their internal nature of self to guide them. Families also relied on the larger, more extended family who resided in the same household for help and guidance. Thus, it appears that the early roots of western psychology were focused on the internal workings of human nature.

As the change took place from hunter-gatherers to the development of industries, work shifted from the home to the factories and plants. A division began to occur between women and men. The choice was made for women to stay at home while men worked outside the home. An emphasis shifted from the more simple and leisurely lifestyle to a busier more competitive drive for material possessions and status. An individual's "self-worth", achievement and accomplishment shifted from that of internal satisfaction to an external drive to acquire possessions, to boast and brag, and to seek external praise and approval for one's accomplishments. Humans were slowly conditioned and trained to believe more and more that the way to attain a higher "self" was through acquiring physical worth, achievement and accomplishments, dollars and bottom lines. Western psychology also shifted from a more internalizing self to an externalizing self; one that can be measured and observed. Human beings began to be studied and compared based on the behaviours they exhibited.

Although there has been a significant shift to redefine psychology to include both mental processes and behaviour, the aim of modern western psychology is still to understand human nature from the outside rather than from the inside or both. Schutz (1969) speaks to the difficult nature of apprehending intended meaning from an individual. He asserts that the comprehension of another's intended meaning could never be achieved and therefore, "the concept of other's intended meaning remains at best a limiting concept." Schutz is not implying that we could never understand another person's experience but rather, the meaning we bring to the experiences of others are not precisely the same as the meaning they themselves hold. He further notes, that we interpret other peoples' meanings based on our own lived experiences and perceptions; a similar concept to existential psychologists. Our explanation for our own lived experiences takes place within the totality of our experience. This totality is made up of all of our encounters with people, places and things (contexts) that we have experienced on our journey to where we are today. To become aware of another's whole experience, we would have to be that person and walk in their shoes in the very same way they walked in them. Hence, Schutz writes, ''everything I know about your conscious life is really based on my knowledge of my own lived experiences (pp. 99,105-107)''. Consequently, to understand human nature, one needs to study and talk to humans and not purely and simply observe their behaviour and actions. For behaviours and actions as Freud puts it, are but mere surface occurrences to more deeper underlying forces that lay beneath the surface.

Existential and humanistic psychologists' view the answers to human nature as existing within themselves (May, 1967). They suggest that the way to learn about humans is to remove ourselves from their stories and let them do the telling, simply and purely. We must be present to the telling or the narratives and not actively try to interpret or perceive or project our thoughts onto them. Human beings are amazingly complex creatures. Each one comes with a distinct and original blueprint, an authentic self which is not like any other and we must all be credited and acknowledged for such.

Self, can be an elusive phenomenon. Sometimes we become aware of it and other times we are not quite sure. Daughters of single mothers, like many other human beings, encounter a variety of experiences which allow them to form impressions and create schemas of the world in which they live. They then perceive and believe these impressions and schemas to be the truth, the "thou shalt" of the world, the way they should behave, what they should believe, and the way things are and should be. They are not yet conscious to the fact that there is a self behind the impressions, the schemas and the conditioning. That very self that propelled them to a higher level of education, resilience, independence and self-reliance. These perceptions often become prescriptions for the way they should act and behave. Issues of trust, modelling, marriage, etcetera, are impressions which led to schemas that were formed along the way based on a particular or a combination of lived experiences. Attaining self, thus, requires one to move beyond his or her strongly ingrained beliefs, based on what they were taught and learned from society, their socialization, to a place of accepting who one is, as one is; and, therefore, accepting others for who they are as well.

Therefore, for the women of this study, coming from the true and authentic self, with all of the good parts and the bad included and to the exclusion of none, will undoubtedly allow them to approach intimate relationships from a place of newness, curiosity, originality and wonderment and with less baggage or preconceived ideas from society of how and why they should or should not be approaching such relationships. They will realize that one does not need the presence of another, namely, a man or partner, to define them and thus become whole or self-actualized but rather a closer examination of oneself, and one's needs. The quality and variety of intimate relationships moving forward may change once they are able to set aside their preconceived notions of what constitutes a healthy sense of self. Once they come to know and accept that the self does not exist outside of them, dressed up like their mother, their father, a man or partner, or a profession or a way of being of behaving or acting, but is a more intimate and personal sense of knowing and longing to be whole that originates within them and that they have choice over, they will realize the deep sense of ownership that they alone have over their life and their existence.

Implications

An interesting observation that was made by the author is that this study presents opposing views to the many studies referenced earlier in the available literature on single parent families. For example, many of the existing studies suggest that children of divorced or separated parents do worse throughout the life cycle. As adults, they are said to have lower educational attainment, earn less, and are more likely to be dependent on the welfare system. They are also said to be more likely to bare children out of wedlock, get divorced and to be the head of a single parent family. Moreover, children who lose their parents through divorce, separation or desertion are said to be vulnerable to acute, psychiatric disturbance as children and as adults (McLanahan, 1995; McLanahan & Burgess, 1988; Glenn & Cramer, 1987; McLanahan, 1988; Amato, 1987; Amato & Keith, 199la; Glen & Cramer, 1985; Tennant, 1988).

Based on the findings of the current study, the portrayal of single parent families noted by the studies above does not appear to paint an accurate and complete picture. Results from this study do not support the notion that children of divorce, separation, desertion, etcetera, are stricken with many of the claims outlined above. For as stated earlier, all of the women in this study were either professionals who are earning a decent living or were striving for such. None of the participants reported relying on the welfare system for support and none reported being divorced or separated. Nevertheless, one of the women did report having a son out of wedlock and another woman saw herself as becoming a single mother because she felt that is what she has always known, what has been modelled for her, and what she is familiar and comfortable with. Moreover, no serious psychological disorders were noted but a more standard need for self-improvement and growth.

Studies describing successful single-parent families indicate that age, maturity level as well as level of education, and level of commitment to the family were contributors to successful single-parent families (Morrison, 1995; Jenkins, 1988; Shireman, 1996). Results from the present study do not support the notion that education level and age contributed to success of the off springs of single-parent families. The majority of the mothers in this study, for example, did not have university or college degrees. Only one of the mothers had a PhD. Some of the other mothers worked in a variety of settings, such as the following: As administrative assistants, home-care worker, at a fish plant, etc. Similarly, most participants indicated that their mothers had them when they were very young and had to support them on their own. At least half of the participants noted that because their moms were young when they had them, their relationship was more like sisters and friends than mother/daughter.

It is important to note and to reiterate that a single experience in one's life does not define who they are; and, rather, it is the multitude and accumulated life experiences that they have had along the way to becoming their present self. Based on the lived experiences of individuals, impressions and schemas are formed which help people compartmentalize and categorize these experiences in order to make sense of and understand their environment. Intimate relating (though an important piece) is still nonetheless, one piece of the greater puzzle that goes into making up an individual's total self. Additionally, it is not fair to assume that because one is raised by a single parent (mother), they will possess certain "undesirable" traits and characteristics.

It should be stated that this author is not intending for the results of this thesis to be representative of all single parent families in the general population. For there are many single parent type families which make up a very diverse cross section of the population. Therefore, this thesis speaks only to the experiences of the females raised in single parent families sampled in this study, grounding the work in the geographic region/ethnic background/class/sexual orientation and religious background in which it was conducted.

For instance, participants in this study were obtained from across two provinces in Eastern Canada, Nova Scotia and Prince Edward Island; two fairly conservative areas with a heavy Christian, religious undertone. In addition, all participants reported coming from a similar socio-economic class and were all Caucasians. Moreover, all participants reported having some post-secondary education and training. Given the nature of the study and the backgrounds from which the participants came, it is likely that their similarities may have contributed to the ways in which they went about answering this study's questions. Further research is needed to look at other aspects of the single parent family. For example, it would be interesting to know whether women raised in other alternative single parenting settings, such as, ethnic/class/sexual orientation, socioeconomic and religious backgrounds, report similar experiences to the women in this study.

Since this is not a large-scale study and because the author is only looking at one type of single-parenting (mother-headed), obtaining a well-balanced group, in terms of when parents became a single unit, was difficult. In addition, the supports single-parents may have received when raising their children may affect the outcome.

Because I have a personal interest in this subject matter and this research serves both as a journey in self-exploration as well as an educational tool, maintaining a reflexive stance throughout was difficult. My interests nevertheless, were the voices of the women under investigation. Therefore, it was important to capture as authentically as possible their own words. The interactions between the participants and the researcher were ongoing; and in order to elicit the quality of information I received from them there had to exist a baseline level of trust, ease and comfort. There was an ongoing sense of fluidity throughout the interviews with the researcher interjecting when needed, seeking clarification, paraphrasing, always going for deeper understanding. As Schutz (1969) notes, it is impossible to capture perfectly what your participants are telling you unless you have walked in their shoes from birth to where they are today. Therefore, my understanding and interpretation of the participants' narratives are based solely on what I bring to the situation to make sense of it.

With most types of research where one seeks to make meaning out of the lived experiences of people, there is usually the reliance on an individual to be truthful or to be as truthful as possible. One cannot be entirely certain whether someone is telling the truth but it was important for the researcher to be fully attentive and alert throughout in order to call into question any inconsistencies or discrepancies that may have arisen.

This study strives to move away from the ongoing stereotyping of single-parent families and to recognize the valiant effort and struggle that go into producing the multitude of perceptions, personalities and diversities within them, that make up their development of self. It gave a voice to six very strong and brave women who represented themselves very well. The voices of these women revealed how socialization and conditioning could shape and mold an individual into becoming something they are not. Their experiences described in this study indicated how perceptions are easily formed based on what we are taught as well as what we are exposed to directly and on the periphery. Positive, healthy parenting of any kind, as well as exposure to positive role models outside of the home, are crucial to the stable development of an individual's sense of self early on their development.

Parenting

The job of parenting is of tremendous importance for a number of reasons. First of all, if parents were to adopt the notion that they are indeed privileged to have been given the opportunity to raise, nurture and affect the development of a human being, an individual's life, especially when not everyone who wants to be a parent gets to be one, there will never be a need to harm or hurt this wonderful, innocent, gentle, soul that lay amidst them. There is no justification in the world that would warrant hurting an innocent child. Being mistreated and treated poorly as a child is not an excuse and does not justify treating children similarly. If anything, that painful lived experience is nothing but a catalyst for righting the wrong. It is an opportunity for redemption, for forgiveness; otherwise, the pattern of negativity, pain, struggle, and abuse will continue to perpetuate itself.

Carl Rogers (1961) was indeed absolutely correct when he said that there was a need for "unconditional positive regard" for children in their early lives. Many have criticized this belief, saying it is too difficult to do because children will inevitably inconvenience or upset their parents by doing something contrary to what they are supposed to be doing. However, does inconveniencing and upsetting one's life, justify placing conditions on the love for a child? For is it not true that these young lives are learning about their environment for the first time and will invariably need to make mistakes in order to learn from them. Gleitman (1991) provided an example of how conditions may be placed on children by using the analogy of, "spilling ketchup on the new living room rug" (p. 734). In this example, suppose a child does indeed spill ketchup on the beautiful cream coloured carpet, does the upset from this incident justify placing the condition of, when you behave properly and not make a mess, only then will you get my love, or be worthy of my love. In essence, a child's self-worth or esteem, in this example is being equated and comparted to the worth of a carpet. A child will grow and develop and later make choices in the world based on what they have learned and observed from their parents, their caregivers, their influencers, but a carpet will eventually get old, and worn, and thrown away. To treat a child as a carpet, is to objectify them, and thus, deal them the same fate as that of the carpet. Children are valuable, but not in the same sense as an expensive rug; their worth is immeasurable and they cannot be replaced.

Significant Others

It is true that significant others can play a tremendous role in children's lives as well. Nevertheless, as noted earlier, significant others formed impressions and developed schemas and perceptions as well, based on what they themselves were exposed to either as children or as adults. If a parent perceives that the way to earn a living is to steal and thus teaches their child to do the same, the child may grow up either perceiving stealing to be the best alternative to earning a living or they may decide that an alternate way is better. Primary caregivers and significant others, however, are not the only means from which children learn, form impressions, develop schemas and thus perceptive the world around them. Friends, relatives, teachers, professionals, strangers, all play a role. A child could have a significant experience outside of the home that changes their lives forever. For example, a child could receive a bad mark on a test, decide it is bad to receive a bad mark and, thus perceives the bad mark to mean they are "dumb". This decision may affect their entire school experience, as they may come to perceive everything they do in life as "dumb". They may continue to perceive themselves in such a way throughout their school experience or they may encounter a teacher along the way who helps them to shift their point of view of themselves, thus changing their schema and perceptions.

Summary

Raising a child under the best of circumstances is perhaps one of the most delicate, important and difficult jobs on the planet. Doing it alone, as a single parent, and as a single mother, can be even tougher; and, so too, is the quest or journey to develop a sense of self for the daughters of single mothers in this study. How we are socialized plays a big part in how we grow and develop. If we are raised to perceive that our sense of self, our worth and well-being come from the things we acquire, display, and see in others, then we will continuously look for and value things outside of ourselves to make us happy. On the other hand, if we are raised to perceive that our sense of self, our worth and well-being come from within us, is native to us, is always with us, is always on our side and can never be taken away from us, our perception of life will be very different. We will feel empowered to change our lives on our terms and not by those forecasted by others. We will eventually come to see that nothing outside of us can make us happy or fulfil us. All of the ingredients of our lives, the experiences, the heartbreaks, the love, the struggle, the triumph, contribute to making and developing our sense of self. However, society's imposition on our lives, its seemingly never ending bombardment of ideas and its many, many ways of representing how to do this or that, make living and navigating through life a more complicated and difficult process for many. Consequently, it is my hope that the richness of information that this study obtained from the remarkable women it studied, will spark further research and insights in this area and continue to represent single parent families in a positive light; not because they deserve to be but because no one deserves to be defined, labelled and judged from the circumstances in which they find themselves.

Appendices

Appendix A
List of Interview
Questions

Background Information

- Tell me about yourself, about who you are at this present time in your life?
- Tell me about your childhood upbringing; what you liked to do or play with, how you spent your time?
- Describe your relationship with your family.
- How long did you live in a single-parent household? How old were you?

- Describe what it was like for you being raised with a single parent.
- Have you ever lived in a household with a man other than your mate, for instance, your father or stepfather, or mother's boyfriend or someone else?
- When was the last time you lived in a house with a male other than your mate?
- What was that relationship like?
- Have you had any male role models in your life on a long term basis, if so, can you describe that relationship to me?

Dating History

- How old were you when you went on your first date?
- How many close relationships have you had since then?
- Do you recall how long these relationships lasted?
- What would you say was the primary cause of your break-ups; who initiated it and what were the circumstances?
- Would you have liked to remain in any of your past relationships if it was possible. If yes, what were your reasons for wanting to stay?
- What would you say are the most important characteristics you look for in a mate, such as, the qualities that mean the most to you or that you value the most?
- What qualities do you dislike the most in a mate and why? How old were you when you went on your first date?

Gender Role Socialization

- Do you feel it is important to have a consistent male as a role model in your life? If yes, what are your reasons? If no, why not?
- How comfortable do you feel when in the company of men socially and intimately?
- How many relationships have you had from the time you were 18 years old to the present? Of those relationships, which ones would you say were the most serious and why?
- Describe your last three relationships for me? How they began, what kept them going, the dynamics of the relationship and how they ended?
- Have you ever considered marriage?
- What are your views on marriage?
- Do you feel that being raised in a single parent household has affected your views on marriage/relationships?

- Would you describe yourself as an independent or dependent person?
- Are you currently involved in a heterosexual relationship?

Demographics

- What type of work do you do?
- What is the highest level of education you have completed?
- What income bracket do you fall into?
  Under -$20,000
  $20,000 -$30,000
  $30,000-$40,000
  $40,000+
- How old are you?

Appendix B
Consent for Discussion
of Interview Material

I, _____

_____ have been informed of the subject matter under investigation by Merryl J. Nash for the purposes of her Master's Thesis. I understand that the Master's Thesis is a requirement for the degree of School Psychology at Mount Saint Vincent University, but may also contribute to the psychological literature from which other psychologists can learn.

I agree to allow discussion of personal material presented in this interview in her Master's Thesis. I understand that several measures designed to protect my confidentiality in this document will be employed. I further understand that I will not be identified by my real name in the Thesis, and other identifying information about me will be disguised.

_____   _____

Participant's Signature   Date

_____

Participant's Name Printed

_____   _____

Researcher's Signature   Date

Appendix C
Consent for Audio Recording of Interview Material

I, _____
have been informed of the subject matter
under scientific investigation by Merryl J.
Nash for purposes of her Master's Thesis. I
have agreed freely, and without influence to
participate in the study and to permit the
audio recording of the interview.

I understand the interview will be audio
recorded for later analysis of the content. I
understand that several measures designed to
protect my confidentiality in this document
will be employed. I understand that the audio
recording of the interview will be destroyed
once the content is transcribed. I further
understand that I will not be identified by my
real name in the thesis and other identifying
information about me will be disguised.

_____   _____

Participant's Signature   Date

_____

Participant's Name Printed

_____   _____

Researcher's Signature   Date

Appendix D
Participant
Consent Form

I,_____
have been informed of the subject matter under investigation by Merryl J. Nash for the purposes of her Master's Thesis. I understand that the Master's Thesis is a requirement for the degree of School Psychologist at Mount Saint Vincent University, but may also contribute to the psychological literature from which other psychologists can learn.

I understand that I will participate in an 1 1/2 hour interview discussing my experiences and opinions regarding being raised in a single parent household and establishing intimate relationships. I understand my participation in this study provides me with an opportunity to potentially make a knowledgeable contribution to the field of psychology and sociology regarding relationships and perhaps more directly to members of my community.

I also realize that discussion of such sensitive issues may evoke some personal emotional upset.

I have freely agreed to participate in the study without influence and I understand that I may freely withdraw my consent at any time without any adverse consequences.

I further understand that several measures designed to protect my confidentiality of participation in the study, and in this document(thesis) will be employed. I understand that the interview will be audio taped and that these audio recordings of the interview will be destroyed once the content is transcribed. I also understand that I will not be identified by my real name in the thesis and other identifying information about me will be disguised.

The researcher (Merryl J. Nash) will provide me with her telephone number and invited me to call with any questions or concerns about the study that may arise from my participation in this study.

I have read the above information and understand the nature of my participation in this study and voluntarily agree to participate.

———————————————   ——————————

Participant's Signature   Date

————————————————————————

Participant's Name Printed

———————————————   ——————————

Researcher's Signature   Date

References

Abelsohnm, D., & Saayman, G.S. (1991). Adolescent adjustment to parental divorce: An investigation from the perspective of basic dimensions of structural therapy theory. *Family process*, 30, 177-191.

Amato, P. R (1995). Single-parent households as settings for children's development well-being, and attainment: A social network/ resources perspective. *Sociological Studies of Children*, 7, 19-47.

Amato, P. R. (1987). Family processes in one-parent, stepparent and intact families: The child's point of view. *Journal of Marriage and the Family*, 49,327-337.

Angel, R., & Worobey, L. J. (1988). Single motherhood and children's health.

Journal of Health and Social Behaviour,
29, 38-52.

Asmussen, L., & Larson, R. (1991). The
quality of family time among young
Adolescents in single-parent and married
families. *Journal of Marriage and the
Family*, 53, 1021-1030.

Atkinson, R. L., Atkinson, R. C., Smith,
Edward, E., & Hilgard, E. R. (1987).
(Ed.). *Introduction to Psychology.* Toronto,
On: Harcourt Brace Jovanovich,
Publishers.

Baker-Miller, J. (1991). The development of
women's sense of self. In J. V. Jordan, J. L.
Surrey, & A. G. Kaplan, *Women's Growth
in Connection: Writings from the Stone
Center* (pp.11-26). New York: Guildford
Press.

Bandura, A. (1977). *Social Learning Theory*.
Englewood Cliffs, New Jersey: Prentice-
Hall, Inc.

Belsky, J. (1981). Early human experience: A family perspective. *Developmental Psychology*, 17, 3-23.

Bempah, J. O. (1995). Information about the absent parent as a factor in the well- being of children of single-parent families. *International Social Work*, 38, 253-275.

Bianchi, S. M. (1995). The changing demographic and socioeconomic characteristics of single parent families. Special issue: Single parent families: Diversity, myths and realities. *Marriage and Family Review*, 20(1/2), 71-97.

Biller, H. B., & Bahm, R M. (1971). Father absence, perceived maternal behaviour, and masculinity of self-concept among junior high school boys. *Developmental Psychology*, 4 (2), 178-181.

Biller, H. B. & Weiss, S. D. (1970). The father-daughter relationship and the personality development of female. *Journal of Genetic Psychology*, 116, 79-93.

Block, J. H., Block J., & Gjerdi, P. (1986). The personality of children prior to divorce: A prospective study. *Child Development*, 57, 827-840.

Borrine, M. L., Handal, P. J., Brown, N. Y., & Searight, H. R. (1991). Family conflict and adolescent adjustment in intact, divorced, and blended families. *Journal of Consulting and Clinical Psychology*, 59 (5),753 -755.

Brown J. H., Portes, P. R., & Christensen, D. N. (1989). Understanding divorce stress on children. Implications for research and practice. *The American Journal of Family Therapy*, 17(4), 315-325.

Butler, B. O., Mellon, M. W. Stroh, S. E., & Stern, H. P. (1995). A therapeutic model to enhance children's adjustment to divorce: A case example. *Journal of Divorce and Remarriage*, 22(3/4), 77-90.

Dornbusch, S. M., Herman, M. R., & Lin, I. C. (1996). Single Parenthood. *Society*, 6, 30-32.

Eggebeen, D. J., Snyder, A. R., & Manning, W. D. (1996). Children in single - father families in demographic perspective. *Journal of Family Issues*, 17 (4), 441-465.

Erikson, E. H. (1968). *Identity: youth and crisis*. New York: W. W. Norton.

Erikson, E. H. (1959). Identity and the life cycle. Psychological Issues, 1, 18-164.

Erikson, E. H. (1950). *Child and Society*. New York, N. Y.: W.W. Norton and Company.

Farber B. N. (1997). Americans all: black single parent families in the inner city. *Ethnic and Racial Studies*, 20(1), 200-209.

Feigelman, W., & Silverman, A. (1981). *Single Parent Adoption*. Administration for Children, Youth, and Families: Washington, D.C., 1-24.

Forehand, R., McCombs, A, Long, N., Brody, G. & Fauber, R. (1988). Early adolescent adjustment to recent parental divorce: The role of interparental conflict and adolescent sex as mediating variables. *Journal of Consulting and Clinical Psychology*, 56(4), 624-627.

Freud, S. (1940). An Outline of Psychoanalysis. Translated by Strachey, J. New York: Norton, 1970.

Freud, S. (1930). Civilization and its Discontent. Translated by Strachey, J. New York: Norton, 1961.

Freud, S. (1917). *A General Introduction to Psychoanalysis*. Translated by Riviere, J. New York: Washington Square Press, 1952.

Fromm, E. (1956). *The Art of Loving*. New York, N. Y.: Harper & Row Publishers, Inc.

Gately, D. W., & Schwebel, A. I. (1991). The challenge model of children's adjustment to parental divorce: Explaining favourable postdivorce outcomes in children. *Journal of Family Psychology*, 5(1), 60-81.

Gilligan, C. (1991). Women's psychological development: Implications for Psychotherapy. *Women and Therapy*, 11, (314), 5-31.

Glasser, B. G., & Strauss, k L. (1 967). The Discovery of Grounded Theory: Strategies for Qualitative Research. Chicago Il: Aldine Publishing Company.

Gleitman, H., (1991). (Eds.) *Psychology*. New York: W.W. Norton & Company.

Gringlas, M., & Weinraub, M. (1995). The more things change: Single parenting revisited. *Journal of Family Issues*,16 (1), 29-52,

Guidubaldi, J., Perry, J. D., & Nastasi, B. K. (1985). Growing up in a divorced Family: Initial and long-term perspectives on children's adjustment. *Divorced Families*, Vol, (1), 202-237.

Hanson, S. M. H., Heims, M. L., Julian D. J., & Sussman M. B. (1995). Single parent families: Present and future perspectives.

Marriage and Family Review, 20 (1/2), 1-25.

Havas, E. (1995). Leading article: The family as ideology. *Social Policy & Administration*, 29 (l), 1-9.

Hetherington, E. M., Stanley-Hagan, M., & Anderson, E. R. (1989). Marital transitions: A child's perspective. *American Psychologist*, 44 (2),303-312.

Hunt, L. G., & Hunt, L.L. (1977). Race, daughters and father loss: Does absence make the girl grow stronger? *Social Problems*, 25, p. 91.

Hyde, J. S. (1996). (Eds.) *Half the Human Experience*: The Psychology of Women. Toronto: D. C. Health and Company.

James, W. (1961). Principles of Psychology. In T. Shipley. *Classics in Psychology* (pp. 151-223.

Jenkins, J. E. (1987). *Creativity: Its Relationship to Single-Parent Family*

Structure. Department of Education: Ithaca, NY, 1-14.

Jung, C. G. (1970). The Development of Personality. *The Collected Works of C. G. Jung*, 17,165-187.

Jung, C.G. (1959). Aion. *The Collected Works of C.G. Jung*, 9 (2), 3-36.

Jung, M. (1996). Family-centered practice with single-parent families. *Families in Society*, 9, 583-590.

Kaplan, A. G., & Klein, R (1991). The relational self in late adolescent. In J. V. Jordan, J. L. Surrey, & A G. Kaplan, *Women's Growth in Connection: Writings from the Stone Center* (pp. 122-131). New York: Guildford Press.

Kapleau, R. P. (1989). *The Three Pillars of Zen*. Toronto, On: Anchor Books, Doubleday.

Kaschak & E. (1992). *Engendered Lives: A New Psychology of Women's Experience*.

New York: Basic Books, A Division of Harper Collins Publishers.

Kornfield J. (1993). *A Path with Heart: A Guide Through the Perils and Promises of Spiritual Life*. Toronto, On: Bantam Books.

Kraft, W. F. (1974). *A Psychology of Nothingness*. Philadelphia, Pennsylvania: The Westminster Press.

Kurdek, L. A & Sinclair, R. J. (1988). Adjustment of young adolescents in two - parent nuclear, stepfather, and mother-custody families. *Journal of Consulting and Clinical Psychology*, 56 (1), 91-96.

Lengua, L. J., Wolchik, S. A, & Braver, S. L. (1995). Understanding children's divorce adjustment from an ecological perspective. *Journal of Divorce and Remarriage*, 25-51.

Leve, L. D., & Fagot B. I. (1997). Gender-role socialization and discipline processes in one-and two-parent families. *Sex Roles*, 36(1/2), 1-21.

Lynn, D. B. & Sawrey, W. L. (1959). The effects of father absence on Norwegian boys and girls. *Journal of Abnormal and Social Psychology*, 18, 258-262.

Maslow, A. H. (1954). *Motivation and Personality*. New York: Harper & Row.

Maslow, A. H. (1968). (Eds.). *Toward a Psychology of Being*. Princeton, N.J: Van Nostrand.

May, R. (1967). *Existential Psychotherapy*. Toronto, On: CBC Publications.

May, R., M., Allport, G. Feifel, H., Maslow, A, Rogers, C. (1961). *Existential Psychology*. Toronto, On: Random House, Inc.

Morrison, N. C. (1995). Successful single-parent families. *Journal of Divorce and Remarriage*, 22(3/4), 205-219.

Muransky, M. J. & DeMarie-Drebow, D. (1995). Differences between high school students from intact and divorced families. Journal of Divorce and Remarriage, 23(3/4), 187-196.

Myers, D. G. (1989). *Social Psychology*. Toronto: McGraw-Hill, Inc.

Oakley, A. (1981a). *Subject women*. Oxford.

Olson, M. R, & Haynes, J. A (1993). Successful single parents. *Families in Society*, 74 (5), 259-267.

Phelps, R. E., & Huntley, D. K. (1985). *Social Networks and Child Adjustment in Single-Parent Families*. Paper presented at the Annual Convention of the American Psychological Association: Rockville, MD, 2-13.

Rogers, C. R. (1942). *Counselling and Psychotherapy: New concepts in practice*. Boston: Houghton Mifflin.

Rogers, C. R. (1961). *On Becoming a Person: A therapist's view of psychotherapy*. Boston: Houghton Mifflin.

Rogers, C.R. (1980). *A way of being*. Boston: Houghton Mifflin.

Rossman, G. B., & Rallis, S. F. (1998). *Learning in the Field: An introduction to qualitative research*. London: Sage Publications.

Samuelson, M. A. K. (1997). Social networks of children in single parent families: differences according to sex, age, socioeconomic status and housing-type and their associations with behavioural disturbances. *Social Networks*, 19, 113-127.

Santrock J. W. (1996). (Eds.) *Child Development*. Toronto: Brown and Benchmark Publishers.

Santrock, J. W. (1970). Paternal absence, sex typing and identification. Development Psychology, 2, 264-272.

Schlesinger, B. (1995). Single parent families: A bookshelf. Marriage and Family Review, 20 (3/4), 463-482.

Schutz A. (1967). The Phenomenology of the Social World Trans. G. Walsh & F. Lehnert.

Seligman, M. E. P. (1975). Helplessness: On Depression, Development and Death. San Franscisco: Freeman.

Spigelman, A., Spigelman, G., & Englesson, I. L. (1994). The effects of divorce on children: Post-divorce adaptation of Swedish children to the family break up: Assessed

by interview data and Rorschach responses. *Journal of Divorce and Remarriage*, 21 (3/4), 171-189.

Spruijt, A. P. (1995). Adolescents from step families, single-parent families and (in) stable intact families in the Netherlands. *Journal of Divorce and Remarriage*, 24 (1/2), 115-132.

Strauss, A, & Corbin, J. (1990). *Basics of Qualitative Research: Grounded theory procedures and techniques*. London: Sage Publications.

Strauss, A, & Corbin, J. (1997). *Grounded Theory in Practice*. London: Sage Publications.

Surrey, J. L. (1991). The self-in-relation: A theory of women's development. In J. V. Jordan, J. L. Surrey, & A. G. Kaplan, *Women's Growth in Connection: Writings from the Stone Center* (pp. 51-56). New York: Guildford Press.

Verna, G.B. (1985). The effects of contextual dissonance of self-concept of you from a high versus low socially valued group. The Journal of Social Psychology, 18, 7-13.

Westkott, M. (1989). Female relationality and the idealized self. *The American Journal of Psychoanalysis*, 49 (3), 249-250.

Wundt, W. (1961). Contributions to the Theory of Sensory Perception. In T.

Shipley. *Classics in Psychology*, (pp. 51-78).

Zaslow, M. J. (1989). Sex differences in children's response to parental divorce. *Orthopsychiatric*, 59 (1), 118-141.

Lightning Source UK Ltd.
Milton Keynes UK
UKHW011821160619
344516UK00001B/177/P